PRAISE FOR STRESS POINT

This book will show young women, who desire to put Christ at the center of their lives, how to live life fully and find godly purpose without compromise. If there's one thing any church leader knows, it's the importance of equipping our 20-somethings with practical ways to invite Jesus into every area of their lives.

> —**Pete Wilson, pastor of Cross Point Church, Nashville, Tennessee and author of *Plan B* and *Empty Promises***

With gracious honesty and girlfriend warmth, Sarah cuts through the drama that often accompanies women in their 20s and offers some of the best advice around. Boy do I wish I would have had this book during those years. *Stress Point* is packed with wonderfully practical application steps, solid scriptural teaching and transparent examples—making this a resource I highly recommend.

> —**Lysa TerKeurst, New York Times Bestselling Author and President of Proverbs 31 Ministries**

Wish you had a road map to navigate your heart through the confusing twenties? Look no further. Sarah Francis Martin nailed it. You are wise to ponder the truths she suggests and, more importantly, put them into practice. I wish I had this book in my twenties. Rest assured, I'll be giving some away. Beginning with my firstborn, Peyton.

> —**Tammie Head, founder of Totally Captivated Ministries, author of *Duty or Delight***

Sarah Martin writes so eloquently what has been in her heart for the past two years. It is with pure joy that I have watched her become the writer she is today. *Stress Point* is the culmination of her God-sized dreams that she has for YOU. Go through each chapter and discover the Kingship of Christ over EVERY area of your life that gives you stress.

> —**Renee Fisher, spirited speaker to the 20-somethings. Author of *Faithbook of Jesus* and *Not Another Dating Book.***

The roaring twenties is a decade of finding out everything about you: who you are, what you'll become and where you'll go. Through *Stress Point: Thriving Through Your Twenties in a Decade of Drama* Sarah Martin comes along with you, leading the way through day to day life. Sarah challenges you to take the top issues in your life and find God's best in each and every one.

—Lynn Cowell, Proverbs 31 Ministries' speakers and author of
His Revolutionary Love

Sarah really taps into the heart of 20-something women in *Stress Point*. For a decade of life that is so full of change and decisions, Sarah has managed to sort through it all and bring hope. To read this book in your 20s (and put her wisdom to work in your life!) is to ensure that you are your healthiest self—physically, emotionally, and spiritually—for many decades to come.

—Annie Downs, author of *Perfectly Unique* (Zondervan, September 2012)

Sarah Martin is the wise, older sister every 20-something needs. With the perfect balance of grace and truth, Sarah tackles relevant issues—and offers practical, biblical truth to move through them with God. If you've been struggling to figure out how to live out your faith in your relationships, your money, even the way you see your body—then Stress Point is the book for you!

—Nicole Unice, student ministry leader, counselor and author of
She's Got Issues (Tyndale, May 2012)

In a time when young adults are becoming increasingly bombarded with the latest trends and tabloids promoting mixed messages about the way we should live, it's no wonder people are stressed! Fresh, relevant, and dashed with a little (or a lot!) of humor, Sarah does an excellent job of engaging her readers with real life issues, while skillfully weaving timeless biblical truths together with practical and personal applications to achieve stress-free living in every area of life. This is a must-read for every college student before heading into the real world!

—Ali Smith, Women's Ministry Director for The Christian Union at Princeton University, author of *Entrusting the Key: From Serial Dating to Joyful Waiting*

STRESS POINT

THRIVING THROUGH YOUR 20S
IN A DECADE OF DRAMA

SARAH FRANCIS MARTIN

THOMAS NELSON
Since 1798

NASHVILLE   DALLAS   MEXICO CITY   RIO DE JANEIRO

Published in Nashville, Tennessee, by Thomas Nelson. Thomas Nelson is a registered trademark of Thomas Nelson, Inc.

Thomas Nelson, Inc., titles may be purchased in bulk for educational, business, fund-raising, or sales promotional use. For information, please e-mail SpecialMarkets@ThomasNelson .com.

Unless otherwise noted, all Scripture references are taken from THE NEW KING JAMES VERSION. © 1982 by Thomas Nelson, Inc. Used by permission. All rights reserved.

Scripture quotations marked AMPLIFIED BIBLE are from THE AMPLIFIED BIBLE: OLD TESTAMENT. ©1962, 1964 by Zondervan (used by permission); and from THE AMPLIFIED BIBLE: NEW TESTAMENT. © 1958 by the Lockman Foundation (used by permission).

Scripture quotations marked ESV are from THE ENGLISH STANDARD VERSION. © 2001 by Crossway Bibles, a division of Good News Publishers.

Scripture quotations marked MSG are from The Message by Eugene H. Peterson. © 1993, 1994, 1995, 1996, 2000. Used by permission of NavPress Publishing Group. All rights reserved.

Scripture quotations marked NIV are from the HOLY BIBLE: NEW INTERNATIONAL VERSION®. © 1973, 1978, 1984 by International Bible Society. Used by permission of Zondervan Publishing House. All rights reserved.

Scripture quotations marked THE VOICE are from The Voice. © 2008 and 2009 Ecclesia Bible Society. Used by permission. All rights reserved.

Library of Congress Cataloging-in-Publication Data

ISBN 978-1-4185-5079-0

Printed in the United States of America

HB 01.16.2018

To Erin, the twentysomething who keeps me real, raw, and relevant. To Greg and Grayson for allowing me time to hang out with my girlfriends and pour out my heart on the pages of this book every Saturday morning. Your support lifted me up when my fingers wouldn't type. Your love filled the gap when I ran on empty. Your encouragement reminded me that God is faithful.

CONTENTS

INTRODUCTION

This book is not about stress. Nope. It would be too easy for you and me to sit around as girlfriends with our coffee cups and chocolate chip muffins venting about the things in our lives that stress us out. That would definitely not be productive. Instead, this book is about life issues common to women in their twenties—stress points—and inviting the King of Kings, Jesus Christ, into the very center of them. Some say that not all stress is bad; a bit of stress in our lives can be a good thing, leading us to action. By recognizing Jesus in all His power and authority and accepting His willingness to be with us at the center of our stress points, issues like money, dating, career, family, friends, and body image will transform from stress points to . . .

godly success,
godly purpose, and
godly well-being.

When we allow Christ to be the center of our lives and involve Him even in the messiest parts we begin to see that God uses the stressful things in our lives to make us more like Him. Isn't it amazing? Here's a phrase that I hope you will be willing and able to wrap your mind around by the end of this book: living out the Kingship of Christ. I know it sounds a bit intimidating and maybe a bit "churchy," but there is great reverence and relevance in this phrase. Once we internalize the concept that Christ is King over all our stress points and is faithful to lead us through them with love and kindness, we look at life with a renewed perspective and increased hope. That's what it means to live out the kingship of Christ. We move from just surviving to thriving in Him.

> *"In the total expanse of human life there is not a single square inch of which the Christ, who alone is sovereign, does not declare, 'That is mine!'"*

—Abraham Kuyper, Dutch Theologian

Jesus, the very One who spoke and the universe appeared, is ready to take your stress over paying bills and declare your bank account, "Mine!"

Jesus, the One and only, who counts every hair on your head, is willing to calm the anxiety over your next job interview and declare your entire career, "Mine!"

Jesus, your loving King, aches for your broken heart and declares your love life, "Mine!"

Jesus, your Abba Father, reaches out to your concern over family drama and declares the relationships, "Mine!"

Girlfriend, let's take this journey together to the throne of the King and allow Him full access to our stress points. Let's let Him lovingly and mercifully claim our issues and daily drama, "Mine!" Let's let Him teach us how to live out the Kingship of Christ without reserving any stress point from His authority.

How to Use This Book

In each chapter you and I will break down our stress points with the following three images of ourselves interacting with Jesus:

Worshiping at the Throne of the King: It is important to celebrate our current circumstances, including our stress points, as we praise God for who He is. In each chapter this segment introduces a different name of God that will elaborate on His character and encourage us to worship through our stress toward more confidence in Christ.

Waiting at the Throne of the King: In times of transition or uncertainty, living out the Kingship of Christ means we simply wait and rest at the feet of Jesus. As you read this segment in each chapter, be prepared to change your definition of the word wait. This is not a time of sitting around idly, but rather a time of being busy in the Bible—gathering wisdom on the stress point at hand.

Finding Focus on the King: Narrow-mindedness is a taboo term in our culture. But in regard to our presence at the throne of the Almighty King, tunnel-vision focus is a must. In each chapter we will zero in on the King, focusing on Him and Him alone is the only way to determine clarity and direction on the ever nagging question, *what is my purpose in life*?

Throughout each chapter we will journal together in Bible study. Although it may be tempting to skip past these blank lines, I sincerely hope you will take the time to work through these journaling opportunities. The Lord will download much truth in our times of interacting with Him, but even more truth is ready for the taking within the Scriptures that are provided in each journaling exercise. I'm excited for you to dig into the verses and converse with God as we work through each chapter and stress point.

At the end of the book I've included an exercise to help you recap how you have grown through our journey together. This will be a spot for you to compile how the Lord has spoken directly to you in each stress point. It can also be a spot to return to for encouragement long after we finish our conversations.

I've lived through my twenties, and I've endured the drama. I know the challenge of leaving home and stepping out on your own for the first time. I know what it's like to live paycheck-to-paycheck, and I remember well the heartache of failed dating relationships. But in the midst of the drama, whenever I have allowed Christ to remain at the center of my stress, I have seen Him grow my character and faith in amazing ways. So when it comes to all the unique challenges you're facing as a 20-something woman, consider me your older girlfriend—someone who has been there and done that; someone to walk with you as you invite Christ into every corner of your life. So as I've mentioned before, this book is not about stress. It is about living life in its entirety with all-out confidence that Jesus is King of Kings and He rightfully declares "Mine!" over our lives. How about we take these stress points and turn them into a thriving, hope-filled journey toward living out the Kingship of Christ?

Grab a cup of coffee and your Bible—I will brew a pot of tea, and let's live it out together!

CHAPTER 1

STRESS POINT:
CAREER
WISHING FOR THAT
DREAM JOB

Nearly every woman in her twenties at some point deals with career woes. We may not be in our dream job at this moment, and we may find ourselves so completely frustrated we'd rather curl up in bed with the comforter over our heads than go to work. But our careers were never meant to be the center of our lives. God planned your career to be a spoke in the wheel of your life, with Him alone as the hub of that wheel. He wants to be not only a reality in your career but the grounding point, the still center to which you come for wisdom, guidance, and godly success. Take a look at these case studies of three 20-something women navigating their careers. Maybe you will see yourself in these examples and take a deep look into your own career situation, evaluating your own top priority.

 ### Girlfriend Case Study #1

Andrea ("Andy") Sachs from the movie The Devil Wears Prada. Andy is a young girl who moves to New York City in the hope of kick-starting a career as a serious journalist. Instead, she ends up as one of two personal assistants to the high-powered editor-in-chief of a top-notch fashion magazine. Andy is professionally and fashionably out of her league in her new job, but she's determined to make it work. Her boss, Miranda Priestly, sees Andy's potential and seems to test her again and again. Andy is frequently instructed to run out-of-control errands and meet impossible deadlines, yet she accomplishes every task with grace and determination, a characteristic that sets her apart from other girls in the office. Miranda notices and takes Andy under her wing. Andy almost loses touch with her dream as she flits around, basking in the glitz and glamour of the fashion world, but a conversation with Miranda jolts her back to reality. As Miranda and Andy sit alone in a limo following a meeting where Miranda has publicly stabbed a friend and colleague in the back, Miranda alludes to the fact that Andy is just like her—a thought that shakes Andy to her core. An interesting exchange transpires, sealing a decision for Andy:

Andy: What if I don't want this?

Miranda: Oh, don't be silly—everyone wants this. Everyone wants to be us.

It is Andy's dream of becoming a professional journalist that ultimately breaks her from the vice grip of Miranda Priestly. At the end of the movie, Andy runs into Miranda on the street, and Miranda doesn't even acknowledge her. Later on, we see Miranda in a limo with a smile on her face, as though to wish Andy well. An interesting note, after standing her ground, Andy ultimately gained Miranda's respect, which lead to an influential recommendation from Miranda to Andy's new employer.

 Girlfriend Case Study #2

Ruth: a beautiful, intelligent, and ambitious career woman. During her college years, Ruth was highly focused and determined to graduate and find a high-powered job. She was the president of her sorority and involved in many campus groups. Once graduation came around, though, Ruth found herself unable to isolate her true passion and translate it into a job.

Interested in world travel, Ruth took a job as a flight attendant, but the events of 9/11 changed circumstances drastically for the airline industry. Finding herself laid off, Ruth bravely packed up and moved from New York City back home to Texas. In the years immediately following, Ruth found herself once again in a state of limbo, uncertain of her passion and direction. Several job opportunities came around, but Ruth always found herself discontent with her situation, and she never stayed in one job for more than a short time. Each one of these job positions could have led her to a successful career, but the waning excitement after a few months in a new job often left Ruth unmotivated and unfulfilled. She recognized that each successive job had taught her valuable skills, and she was grateful for the experience; yet Ruth found herself continuously on the lookout for the "next best thing." She was searching endlessly for a dream job that she had not yet defined.

Girlfriend Case Study #3

Sarah (Me): a sales representative who focused in on one area of interest and landed her dream job by the age of twenty-four. During my senior year of college I aspired to find a sales position and worked hard to realize this goal. When I wasn't in class, working, or socializing, I spent most of my extra time researching the sales industry and networking. Although I was told by a recruiter at a college career fair that I wasn't ready to take on this type of job, I was determined that one day I would be. Several years later I did in fact find myself working for a large sales company and loving life. Day in and day out I thrived on successful sales calls, and the company rewarded me nicely for my passion and intensity. My whole world revolved around this dream job—it had become my passion. I lived for this dream job, but at what expense?

5/18/2018

Journal 1
IDENTIFY YOURSELF

- With which of the case study girlfriends do you most identify, and why?

I identify most with Ruth because I am having a hard time isolating what my passions are & translating it to a job. I find myself in a state of limbo & wonder if I should stay or go.

- In what ways is your career or your pursuit of a career stressing you out these days?

These days, I'm stressing over staying at this job or moving onto a new job to figure out if accounting is what I can do & like.

- Are you presently working at your dream job? If not, describe that job.

I don't think I am right now. I think I desire to gain confidence in this profession and I like some aspects of it, but I'm not sure if I love it. My dream job would be to either own a business or use my communication skills to guide others. Like in counseling or human resources.

Worshiping at the Throne of the King

No matter what stage of our career we currently find ourselves in or what level of enthusiasm we bring to our job, we're called to worship our Lord in every situation. But if I'm stressing about my job, or the lack thereof, I would prefer to mope around in my jammies, feeling sorry for myself. When I'm experiencing career issues, it is difficult for me to find the energy just to lift my hands in praise. *withdraw/depletion ——→ Worship*

Together in this book we will look at different names of God that shed light on His character. In the Old Testament especially, the Hebrews used names of God to display His character as a means of telling how God spoke to them or acted on their behalf. Out of all the names of God, this one speaks to me during stressful times at work: *El Elyon*, the High and Powerful. Look with me at Psalm 7:17. Knowing that I worship the almighty God who created the universe and everything in it assures me that He has everything under control, including my career. David, the author of Psalm 7, could shout God's name in a loud, grateful song because he knew God as his El Elyon—his God Most High.

> I will praise the LORD according to His righteousness, and will sing praise to the name of the LORD Most High. (Psalm 7:17)

David praised the Lord as El Elyon to put his heart in the right place— to remind himself that God is above all. Over and over again in the Psalms and throughout the rest of Old Testament, we see Scripture that reminds us there is no other God but our almighty Creator, El Elyon. Also, as the name El Elyon suggests, the Lord knows you inside and out, so much so that He maintains a tally sheet of the numbers of hairs on your head at any given moment. El Elyon calibrated the human DNA system in a specific way just for you, in order to affect your particular personality and physical traits. As the Most High, He has your career under control, with all of its twists and turns worked out. *Why doesn't He just let me go at it and allow me to work at something I'm passionate about?* you might ask. What you may not be factoring in is that the Lord uses times of waiting to build patience and perseverance. God, your El Elyon, wants the best for you. You can give Him your best in anticipation by acknowledging that you're blessed with unique gifts and by being patient to wait on His timing for how your dream job might play out.

But what if your original dream job doesn't turn out to be all it was cracked up to be, yet you have no idea what you'd rather be doing? As our girlfriend Ruth struggled with dissatisfaction, she continuously placed her dreams in the Lord's hands. But what, specifically, does that mean? When we lay our worship and praise at God's feet and work to please Him, He'll work out the logistics for attainment of that dream job. If you dream and wish for that perfect job to come your way, steer your focus right to the throne of your King, your El Elyon. Our dreams might emcompass a fleeting moment or desire, but our ultimate wish should be the glory and purposes of the Lord. By worshiping Him in our job situations, whether or not the circumstances are ideal, we run smack dab into happiness, blessings, and fulfillment. Dissatisfaction in our jobs is enveloped and overridden by insatiable satisfaction in El Elyon—our one and only Wish.

What does the following verse say to you personally, with regard to your career?

> I will cry out to God Most High, to God who performs all things for
> me. (Psalm 57:2)

God knows your dreams, but He wants to be your one and only Wish. He wants you to run to Him with your job woes, so He can scoop you up in His strong arms and console you with His wisdom, love, and peace. Take time right now to worship your God Most High and to thank Him, both for the gifts He has freely given you and for the future that is yet to unfold. I encourage you to approach the throne of the King daily, maybe even hourly (if need be), as well as to take the time to worship God for being your Most High—the One who has your life, your career, and your dreams under control and running on course.

Journal 2
I WILL WORSHIP AT THE THRONE

In your Bible read through Jeremiah 29:11–14 several times.

• Verse 11 states that God knows the plans He has for you. Not infrequently, the Lord chooses to leave us in the dark for a while with regard to our future, and that includes our future career. Does it freak you out to recognize that He knows the plan for your career even when you don't? Why or why not?

_____

_____

_____

_____

• If our relationship with the Lord isn't such that we can trust Him in the midst of uncertainty, these verses might drive us nuts. Are you in a place where you find yourself able to trust God, in particular with your job? Why or why not?

_____

_____

_____

_____

- We've talked about acknowledging the skills and talents God has given us and thanking Him for them, even while we wait to use them in our dream job. Now would be a good time to take an inventory. Write out a list of your talents, whether or not you see them as specifically work-related.

_____

_____

_____

_____

- When was the last time you took a hard look at your gifts and made a plan to actually use them? If it has been a while, or if you've never taken this step toward planning, I encourage you to do so now. (God doesn't object to our planning, so long as we acknowledge Him as the One in charge.) In the space below write down some things you plan to do in order to use your gifts.

_____

_____

_____

_____

Waiting at the Throne of the King

You probably cheered for our girlfriend Andy as she stepped away from the glamorous job at the fashion magazine, because you knew the job didn't fit her passion and dreams. Yet even during her period of waiting, Andy observed, learned about the industry, and made the best possible use of her opportunities to grow and network. She took the job at the fashion magazine as a stepping stone, and it ultimately gave her great experience and connections to move on to her dream job. She knew where her passions lay, and she took concrete measures to move toward a job as a legitimate journalist. Though her time at the fashion mag wasn't always fun, the end goal was always at the front of her mind.

Do you find yourself, like Andy, in a position of limbo right now? Keep in mind that most people in their early twenties don't step off the college graduation platform directly into their six-figure dream job. Most of us have to pay our dues, putting in time in jobs that give us meaningful experience but barely give us enough money to pay the bills! This period may be considered almost a rite of passage, not to mention an important moment in which to practice waiting on God and submitting to His timing for our career path.

This type of waiting needs to be proactive, involving much more than clocking in at work and wishing each day away. On the contrary, God intends this waiting period to be a productive type of waiting, in terms of acquiring and honing skills while developing abilities you may already possess. During our time of waiting at the throne of the King, we're to grow in our prayer life and Bible knowledge as we listen to Him speaking truth to us about the direction He has for our lives—including our careers. This truth may not be easy to swallow. Maybe the Lord wants you to step off into a different career path from the one you've imagined since you were young. Maybe He wants this time of waiting to strengthen your character so that you'll grow into a woman of integrity and grace for your upcoming job. There can be no doubt that this period of waiting at the throne can, at first glance, appear to be a waste of time. But if God has an amazing plan for you, don't you want to be fully equipped not just to handle it but to succeed in it? Look at this waiting period as a time of refinement, and you'll be rewarded later on for your patience.

We discussed Jeremiah 29:11–14 in Journal 2, but I'd like to revisit this passage and focus specifically on verses 13 and 14. These verses are often found on cute little placards and fridge magnets. The problem is that we tend to skim this significant passage, failing to take it to heart with regard to our stress points. Take a moment to reread these verses in the context of waiting at the throne with regard to your career:

> For I know the thoughts that I think toward you, says the LORD, thoughts of peace and not of evil, to give you a future and a hope. Then you will call upon Me and go and pray to Me, and I will listen to you. And you will seek Me and find Me, when you search for Me with all your heart. I will be found by you, says the LORD. (Jeremiah 29:11–14a)

Seek the Lord in the uncertainty of unemployment. Seek the Lord in your dysfunctional relationship with your coworkers. Seek the Lord as you step up the career ladder. Seek the Lord as you develop important job skills. Seek the Lord when you just can't seem to drag yourself out of bed to face another day in that cubicle. And when you do, you'll find Him— guaranteed. When you wait before Him and get to know His strength, power, and love, He'll reveal His plans for you. They'll be amazing, so stick close and obey. The verses above promise that His plans are to prosper you and give you a future, one in which you can be fulfilled no matter what job you have at the moment. Just keep in mind that it all starts with seeking Him and taking a seat at the foot of the throne.

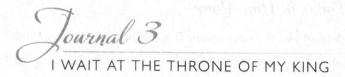

I WAIT AT THE THRONE OF MY KING

Soak in these verses from Psalm 16.

> LORD, you have assigned me my portion and my cup; you have made my lot secure. The boundary lines have fallen for me in pleasant places; surely I have a delightful inheritance. (Psalm 16:5–6)

• I look to this verse not only in times of doubt about my own life situation but also in times of jealousy over others' circumstances. I cling in particular to the part that says, "You have assigned me my portion" (v. 5). This reminds me that it is God who has placed me where I am in my life in terms of my career, relationships, friendships, money, etc. In which areas of your career (or other aspects of your life) do you wish your situation was more like someone else's? Be specific.

_____

_____

_____

• Godly success is achieved when we work our tails off within whatever position God has currently placed us. Psalm 16 says that the boundary lines have "fallen" for you. I would define boundary lines as where God has you at this moment right now. It isn't by accident that you find yourself at your present job. Can you find pleasure where your boundary lines have "fallen" for you at this point? Where are you *right now*, and can you be happy and content?

_____

_____

Finding Focus in Him Alone

I have a tendency toward tunnel vision. This can be a positive trait when I'm working against a deadline or while I'm in the midst of a job hunt. However, when I wear my blinders my focus quickly turns away from the Lord. As I mentioned in our girlfriend case study, my dream job in sales consumed my life. I spent hours at night responding to emails, preparing for the next workday and researching industry trends. Not until late in the evening would I finally surface, only to notice that I had neglected house-work, my fitness routine, and my loved ones. This really didn't bother me, however, since I had my work-tunnel-vision blinders trained forward and upward along the trajectory of my career path. As women, after all, don't we sometimes feel as though we have to prove ourselves just to keep up with the men? This perspective only fueled my intensity, which, I recognize in hindsight, often turned my coworkers off.

A narrow focus on our dream job isn't necessarily bad. Some of us are highly driven, and this serves us well. The problem comes in when we neglect the big-picture life with which God has blessed us, and instead go for climbing the career ladder or obtaining that holy grail of a dream job. In the end, living life with God in our sights is all about worshiping Him, serving Him, and balancing the rest of our life (including our career) in conformity to His direction. This happens when we train our focus on Him alone. Not on our job. Not on our paycheck. Not on our next career move. On Him *alone*.

The Lord spoke to my heart on this issue and set me straight. I needed balance in my career life. Prior to this, I'd been all about my job. Then one day during my Bible study a verse jumped out at me, and I found myself unable to backpedal away from it:

Whatever you do, work at it with all your heart, as working for the Lord, not for men, since you know that you will receive an inheritance from the Lord as a reward. It is the Lord Christ you are serving. (Colossians 3:23–24 NIV)

"As working for the Lord . . ." *Whoa there!* Have you ever had a Bible verse smack you in the face? This one smacked me and alerted me to a cold, hard truth. I wasn't seeking to please the Lord with my work; instead, I was laboring to collect a fat bonus, to impress my boss, and to boost my self-esteem. After a while I realized that although this job was itself a gift from God, I was never intended to place my whole world around it. True and meaningful success comes when I work my butt off to please the Lord alone. But there's a fine line I cross when I live with, in, and through my work as though my life depended on it. Here are a few ideas to help you maintain balance in your life with regard to your career:

- ❧ If you're passed over for a promotion, keep in mind that you are to continue to work hard and to develop a plan for the next promotion. This isn't the end of the world.

- ❧ Bring balance to your work schedule by spending quality time alone with Jesus. Whether that happens before you start your workday, during your lunch break, or in the evening, consistency is key. Day-to-day communication with God points your focus in the right direction.

- ❧ Remember that your paycheck, or the lack thereof, doesn't define your worth. If you've worked to please the Lord, that's all that matters. You are worthy of Him, and He loves you dearly.

- ❧ Pray throughout the day. It's so easy to get caught up in office gossip or a customer crisis, while forgetting to bring it all to Him in prayer. The Holy Spirit doesn't shy away from giving us guidance, even in our career.

- ❧ Be a light pointing your coworkers toward the Lord. If we live as though our life revolves around work rather than around Him, how does this look to our coworkers? Do they even know we're Christians when we behave this way? I shudder to think back on the days when my boss and partners didn't even know I worshiped the King of Kings. My real worship was directed toward my job, which greatly disappointed the Lord. Balance and priority are keys to a life of godly success in the workplace.

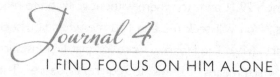

I FIND FOCUS ON HIM ALONE

- Let's check back in with Jeremiah 29 in regard to our focus on the Lord. Read it over again in your own Bible. Verse 11 says that God plans to prosper you and give you hope. The word "prosper" might stand out to you while you are working with Him on your career, since work and money go hand in hand. God's version of "prosper" is different than what we often think of the word. When God prospers us, He prospers us holistically. This means that we have a wealth of hope, peace, joy, patience, and love. (See what Galatians 5 has to say about the fruit of the Spirit.) He prospers us with a rich relationship with Him; a relationship in which we can come to the throne and experience His greatness. Sometimes the word prosper refers to financial gain, but this is not the main goal of the Lord. He wants us to be wealthy in our trust and faith in Him alone. What areas in your life do you need to be more prosperous in the Lord?

- We often read Jeremiah 29:11 and stop there without going on to read verse 13, which says, "You will seek me and find me when you seek me with all your heart" (NIV). The Hebrew word for that first instance of "seek" is *baqash*, which means "to seek, to require, to desire." The second instance of "seek" is a different Hebrew word, *darash*, which means "to resort to or to search." When we desire God and resort to His direction, He will be found; that is a promise. To seek and to search means to actively pursue God by reading His Word and spending quality time in prayer. Do you desire God's direction for your career, or are you holding on to the reins yourself?

- Do your career goals line up with seeking, desiring, and searching for God?

Stress Diverted

Take some time to set specific, achievable goals toward your dream. Once you've sought the Lord and come to trust Him with the direction of your career, you can truly align your goals with His purpose. Before you begin assessing your career goals with the Lord in mind, ask yourself these questions:

- ✿ After spending time in prayer and in the Bible, have I found clear direction from God for my career path?

- ✿ Does my dream job coincide with where I sense God to be leading me? If not, am I willing to lay my dreams aside, knowing that what God has planned is better?

- ✿ What professional steps do I need to take to move in this new direction?

- ✿ What mentors has God placed in my life? Will they hold me accountable in my quest for this new career direction?

Once you've answered these questions, start setting short-term goals. Make it an objective to revamp your résumé, search for jobs that will afford you quality experience, and attend community networking events. Establish an exact time frame during which to achieve these short-term goals. Then, determine your long-term goals. This will be a running list that will continue to evolve as you accomplish your short-term tasks. Continually ask yourself at every step in the process, *Does this conflict with the Lord's direction for my career? Am I manipulating matters in my own way?* If you veer off God's road, scratch that goal off the list or go at it from a new angle, acknowledging that His way is better.

God never intended for us to stress and obsess about anything, not even our careers. Through our approach to the throne in worship, in waiting and in focusing on Him alone, we lay down our concerns about our dream quest and take up the assurance that the Lord knows and cares about our desires. In worship we find ourselves content in every situation, even if we aren't in our dream job just yet. Through the wait, our present circumstances, both positive and negative, can become a time of meaningful growth. With our focus on Jesus, we achieve our dreams because we're working for Him alone. All three practices—worshiping, waiting, and finding focus on the Lord—will bless you and keep you in His plan for your life. This plan is far more exciting than anything you could ever imagine.

Waiting at the throne and training our focus on Jesus isn't always fun and exciting; we might find ourselves frustrated and ready to give up. At that point, conversation with the Lord will spark our attention and get us back on track. The key isn't to check "prayer" off your to-do list and move on with our day. It's to reconnect with the Lord and wait in patient expectation before His throne. Your El Elyon takes delight in continuous dialogue with you over your stress points, so tap into His wisdom for your career.

Journal 5

I LAY IT ALL DOWN BEFORE THE THRONE

Below are some prayer point journal prompts. Finish these thoughts with your own words in a written prayer.

- *Lord, my El Elyon, I know that my dreams are important to You. Help me make You my Wish. Show me first of all what this means . . .*

- *Father, these are the particular areas in which I'm dissatisfied with my present career . . .*

- *Lord, I acknowledge that You are the Most High God and that You're ever present, even in my career. I worship You . . .*

- *My El Elyon, I wait at Your throne with my dreams. Teach me . . .*

- *God, I long for You and You alone to be my priority and my focus. Show me the areas in which I'm falling short of this lifelong goal.*

---

*Go to **www.liveitoutblog.com/stress-point** to watch a video from Sarah on this chapter's Stress Point!*

CHAPTER 2

STRESS POINT:
SELF-IMAGE
COMFORTABLE
IN MY OWN SKIN

I once heard Dr. Phil make a snarky remark to a guest on his show that stayed in my mind and migrated to my heart the next time I found myself struggling with my self-image and traveling down the familiar road of beating myself up. He said, "You wouldn't worry so much about what people thought of you if you knew how seldom they did." Ouch. Let's think about that for a second. You mean, other people are so worried about themselves that they rarely think twice about me? Yes!

This quote helps me realize I have permission not to stress over the opinions of others; instead I can focus on what God thinks of me and where I stand in His eyes. In this chapter's three girlfriend case studies, you will notice how each girlfriend differs in her self-image and how each one deals with the same junk as you and me. We all learn how to be comfortable in our own skin in different ways, but take heart and know that you are not alone in your insecurities and fears.

Girlfriend Case Study #1

Betty Suarez from the TV show *Ugly Betty*. Betty walks into the high fashion magazine, *MODE*, with a sweet confidence. The camera pans to capture the horror on her coworker's faces as Betty strolls in wearing a leopard print vest coupled with a hot pink blouse —yes, blouse—and hot pink pumps. Betty doesn't seem to notice their stares as she sits down at her desk ready to start her day. Her snooty colleagues often coach her on what to wear to best flatter her not-so-slim figure, and she takes it all in stride. But all of the disdain from Betty's high fashion "friends" doesn't seem to change who she is or even her style, for that matter. Before jumping into an editorial meeting to discuss the next month's layout, Betty fiddles with the large pendant hanging from her neck in the shape of a B. This is the signature piece she wears day after day regardless what outfit she has on. She treasures this piece of jewelry because it reminds her to stay true to who she is no matter the latest fashion craze. Just as Betty is about to walk into the big meeting, she phones her father to touch base. Although her pendant is a good reminder, Betty's family are the ones who really keep her grounded. They helped shape the smart, confident woman she has become, and they push her to stay true to who she really is when the magazine tempts her to change her style. What makes Betty so relatable in this television show is how she clings tight to who she is. Her personal style—albeit counter to the magazine's culture—serves as encouragement for us to live out our lives as true to how God made us. Betty refuses to be swept up in the ever-changing fashion environment.

 ### Girlfriend Case Study #2

Renee, a sweet and beautiful 20-something new Christian. Just months after accepting Jesus as Lord, Renee meets a little-bit-older, really cute, God-loving man who lives in her apartment community. We'll call him

Mike. They start dating, and Mike sweeps Renee off her feet with notes that include pieces of Scripture for encouragement and chivalrous acts such as asking permission to hold her hand. Soon, Mike puts a ring on Renee's finger, and they start making plans for the wedding. Two weeks after proposing, Mike decides that Renee is not the woman for him. She's devastated, wondering what is so wrong with her that he'd changed his mind. Renee Swope shares this story in her book *A Confident Heart*, about how she has struggled all her life with fear of abandonment due to her father leaving when she was a toddler. After Mike leaves, Renee is convinced that she just isn't "worth staying for." Eventually, God picks up the pieces of Renee's broken heart, and before long she starts letting guys get within twenty feet of her again. Soon after, Mike comes back into her life, and Renee forgives him. They start dating again, get engaged, and four weeks later Mike dumps her again. This time Renee keeps the ring and insists she and Mike see a counselor. During this time, Renee happens upon Mike's journal. She's fully aware these are private thoughts of Mike's and the words are not meant to be seen by anyone; she knows her own journal has pages she'd rather no one read. But Mike's journal sits in front of her, beckoning Renee to look inside. When she does, she discovers that, according to Mike, she's "too strong willed." Even worse, she's "not tall enough, skinny enough, or good enough"—things she has believed and feared all her life. The relationship ends, and Renee walks away feeling inadequate, rejected, and abandoned. In her book she says something we all might relate to in regard to rejection and dealing with other's opinions of us: "After reading Mike's journal, every time I saw a beautiful woman or stood in front of a mirror, doubt whispered, 'No man will ever want you.'"[1]

 Girlfriend Case Study #3

Kristen, a single twenty-eight-year-old talented high school English teacher. As is her daily routine, before Kristen walks out the door for school, she logs onto Facebook. Kristen spots a picture in her newsfeed that catches her attention. She didn't know that her friend Kerri took a trip to the Bahamas! How does a first-year law student afford such an extravagant vacation? Kristen can't help but click through Kerri's Facebook album, and her heart sinks as she locks eyes on the super-hot guy Kerri is hugging while wearing an itty bitty bikini that looks fantastic on her. Suddenly all of Kristen's hard work on the treadmill every night seems insignificant as she obsesses over her friend's perfect figure. Kristen glances at her watch and freaks out. What should have been a few minutes on the computer turned into twenty minutes, and now she is late for work. As Kristen drives to school, she thinks to herself, *Why does everyone else but me have this perfect life? Why am I the only one who doesn't have a husband or even a boyfriend? Is there something wrong with me? Am I not worthy of such a beautiful life?*

Journal 1

IDENTIFY YOURSELF

- Which of the women in the case studies do you identify with in regard to how you view yourself?

- What does the dialogue in your head sound like when you think about your self-image and how others view you?

- If that dialogue is a negative one, let's work through that in this chapter. Do you see the value in bringing this stress point, your self-image, to the throne of your King? How do you need Him to speak to you today about this stress point?

Worshiping at the Throne of the King

Celebrities are often asked in interviews how they "stay grounded." This phrase is a chic way of talking about how to stay focused and not get wrapped up in the hype of celebrity life. Because this phrase is somewhat illusive to me, I decided to Google it. After sifting through pages and pages of Web sites with mystical, self-aggrandizing messages to get to the bottom of what "grounded" means, I've decided that, plain and simple, and in keeping with the quote from Dr. Phil that is forever engrained in my brain, we all just need to get over ourselves!

What I love about our girlfriend Betty is that she truly loves her curves, her braces, her quirky style, and her roots—where she comes from. Betty knows who she is and who she is not. And I bet her coworkers secretly wish they were that confident and self-assured. Have you ever met someone who floats into the room with a certain ease and wondered, what does she have that the other women in the room lack? If so, you are not alone. Most women are searching for that calm, assured security in themselves. In fact, every month, more than 6.5 million readers pick up the magazine titled SELF.[2] This health and fitness mag touts expertise in areas of toned butts, perfectly conditioned hair, and the keys to happiness. It's all about self. As a 20-something, you might very well be poring through these types of magazines, searching for answers on how to figure out just who you really are. You might feel like you just aren't comfortable in your own skin—not completely insecure like you were in that awkward, junior high stage, but still not self-assured and confident. It's important to be easy on yourself and remember that this is a transitional decade in which you have your whole life ahead of you, yet you're still carrying the baggage from your past.

I often lay in bed and recall the awkward moments of my teenage years when the cool girls snubbed me and the boys cracked blonde jokes in front of a classroom of insecure thirteen-year-olds. As my brain digs deeper into those memories, I can't help but relive the exact words that instigated the blonde jokes. I was a good student, but sometimes I just didn't use my head. During school I often spoke out loud before I thought out my comment, and I ended up sticking my foot in my mouth. There is one particular memory that plays over and over in my head. I sat in English class having just turned in a kickin' paper entitled "God's Just Not Finished with Me Yet." I cannot recall the question asked by the teacher, but my answer was dumb . . . really dumb. The whole class laughed, and one particularly loudmouthed, pimply faced guy called me an airhead. Holding back the tears long enough for the bell to ring, I gathered my purse and my stack of pink-covered textbooks and bolted out of the classroom, but not before noticing the "cool" girls laughing and whispering in my direction.

Lying in my bed in the dark of night many, many years later, the embarrassment still plagues me. It is only in the last few years that I've learned that those memories do not define me. What is so interesting about this memory is that though I don't remember the specific question from the teacher or the "dumb" answer I gave, the feelings of insecurity have stuck with me for many years. Now I realize, though, that I am not that thirteen-year-old "airhead" any longer. This level of maturity in my self-image only comes with an assurance in knowing just who my Majestic King is, just who it is that created me, and who I am because of His magnificence.

I use the name Majestic King in this chapter more as a description than as a technical name of God. The words *majesty* and *majestic* are sprinkled beautifully throughout the Bible, and I've really latched on to this characteristic of God! Merriam-Webster defines *majesty* as "sovereign power, authority, or dignity" and "greatness or splendor of quality or character."[3] I love the regal nature of these defining words and can't help but imagine God as all powerful and majestic.

Worship with me at the throne of the Majestic King. Let's turn away from our self-focus, which is not true reality. We were not created to obsess over finding who we are. Instead, we were created to worship and immerse our entire selves in the Lord, who is full of glory and majesty. Wrapping our self and our identity in Jesus takes time and effort on our part, and that includes worshiping Him for His majesty and recognizing how our self fits into the concept of His greatness. When we stop obsessing over simply finding who we are, we are able to focus our energy and worship on evaluating who we are in relation to who Jesus is. This is where our true identity comes into play. This is where it is okay to look inside and ask, *Am I reflecting Jesus in a way that brings glory to Him? Or am I always worried about what other people think of me?*

Psalm 8 works as a pep talk for me to rev up my worship of my Majestic King. Do you ever take moments out of your day to acknowledge the beauty around you? I personally envy David, the psalmist, who recognized the splendor the King chooses to let us participate in. David unabashedly shouts this praise to God:

> When I consider Your heavens, the work of Your fingers,
> The moon and the stars, which You have ordained,
> What is man that You are mindful of him,
> And the son of man that You visit him?
> For You have made him a little lower than the angels,
> And You have crowned him with glory and honor. (Psalm 8:3–5)

At the same time David worships in the assurance that he has the privilege to approach the throne of his Majestic King, David poses questions that make us consider where we stand with God. Asking questions is a natural part of life, and verse four serves as a searching question and an affirming statement of what exactly David believes about God. This psalm helps us to worship who God is and who we are in relation to His majesty. We can ask, "Who am I that You, Lord, care about me? Who am I that You, who gently whispers and a rainbow forms, would love and adore me so dearly? Who am I that You would forgive me day after day for living wrapped up in myself rather than wrapping myself up in who You are?

Take a few minutes to work through the following journal segment to unpack who exactly you are based on the Majestic King you serve.

Journal 2
I WILL WORSHIP AT THE THRONE

One day as I read through Psalm 95 in conjunction with Psalm 8 (which is mentioned in the previous section), I felt the Lord answer the question posed in Psalm 8:4: *Who am I, Lord, that you care about me?* I've shared my thoughts below . . .

Who am I? I am the one who Jesus considered when forming my favorite spot on the shoreline of my favorite beach.

Who am I? He smiled and thought of me when designing the Gerber daisy—knowing pink would thrill my soul.

Who am I? As He fashioned the seeds of the strawberry, Jesus foresaw my taste for all things sweet and juicy.

Read Psalm 95 and Psalm 8 before you write your own answers to the question, *Who am I?* Your turn . . .

Who am I?

_____

_____

Who am I?

_____

_____

Who am I?

_____

_____

Waiting at the Throne of the King

I heart Facebook. I really, really do. In fact, as I'm typing this with my venti iced green tea at my local Starbucks, I couldn't resist the urge to check out what all my friends were up to before I returned to writing this chapter. It is like watching a mindless reality TV show; I just can't turn away! Can you relate to our sweet teacher-friend Kristen in the case study earlier in this chapter? Are you one of those people who pore over all of their Facebook friends' pictures and updates? I sure am one of those people, and sometimes all of that "Facebook stalking" does nothing to help my self-esteem. In general, are you one to think about all of your friends with boyfriends, fiancés, children, and dream houses and ask, *When is it my turn? What is wrong with me that I don't have all these great things?*

Waiting at the throne of our Majestic King means we are comfortable where God has us at this very moment. Waiting also means that we are honest about our circumstances. Whether in conversations with our coworkers or in our status updates on Facebook, waiting means authentically showing who we are in light of a merciful and majestic King. This means we allow Him to shine His light on our deep, dark, not-so-cute hearts and let people know what we are really dealing with as well as how God is dealing with it along with us. You and I can't do that if we sugarcoat our lives to look like what we think people will appreciate and accept.

In addition, when we are vulnerable and real, this gives others permission to be real, too. True connection and ministry happen when someone else knows they are not alone, because we've shared our own struggles. It can be a chain reaction: we share our heart and give someone else encouragement to do the same, they go and let someone else know of a struggle, that person in turn shares their heart, and so on until there's a bit of healing in heart after heart, simply because you were real and raw.

I'd like to issue you a challenge. I'm going to call it the Facebook Challenge, but this absolutely applies to our lives outside of Facebook as well—our "in real life" lives. Without being overly negative or sharing too many personal details, for the next week I challenge you to be real in your conversations and/or your Facebook status. It is always interesting for me to see how my friends react when I spill my guts. Take a peek at one convo I started via a Facebook status I posted not too long ago:

Sarah: Learning a hard lesson today: extending grace is not optional or good to do only "when I feel like it." It is imperative. Ouchie.

Kathleen: You hit me right between the eyes!! Thanks!!!!

Sarah: Ha! Sorry! Just passing along what the Lord smacked me over the head with this morning! :)

Kathleen: I'm sure it was meant for me, too!!! It's no accident that I read your post!!!! LOL

So are you up for the challenge? Go for it. Be real. Be raw. Do ministry and make connections by simply sharing your heart. Set a foundation among your community of friends, family, and coworkers in which everyone is authentic and willing to share struggles. This is like a clean canvas whereon one person adds a dab of color (what they are feeling), another person touches up the canvas with a bit of ink (what makes them tick), and yet another person turns the piece into a collage by adding a bit of paper (their doubts or fears). Soon, a beautiful piece of art forms as God uses His creativity to make the art—the community of people—magnificent and authentic.

Journal 3
I WAIT AT THE THRONE OF MY KING

Take some time to read through what might already be a familiar passage to you, Mark 4:1–9. In light of our discussion on authentically portraying ourselves based on God's majestic character, break down the three types of soil Jesus refers to in this parable and what happens to each one. Let's consider that the soil (stony ground, thorns, good soil, etc.) represents our character—our very openness to God's love. The seed represents God's Word: His love, what He teaches us about Himself, and who we are in relation to Him.

• Thinking in terms of character and authenticity, what do you think is the difference between good soil and bad soil?

_____

_____

_____

_____

• How does God interact with each type of soil? How does each type of soil listed in the passage reflect good, bad, or shady character?

_____

_____

_____

_____

- Journal out some ways that you can live authentically in light of who God made you to be. How does good soil yield a fruitful crop? (Hint: see verse 8.) How can you best cultivate the character and personality God gave you to portray His majesty in your life?

Finding Focus on Him Alone

Were you intrigued by Renee's story about her fiancé and his journal? I sure was. Renee's story continues in her book, *A Confident Heart*, where she lets us know that she has made amends with Mike. In fact, they later attended one another's weddings. And although she and Mike have come to a place of healing and are able to maintain a friendship, Renee suffered a hurt heart, and her self-image took a beating. In her book she describes how Satan uses various circumstances and the opinions of others to bring us down. She says, "He [Satan] knows if he can paralyze us with self-doubt and insecurity we will never live up to the full potential of who we are and what we have in Christ."[4] I love that! Amen, Sister! Who we are in Christ, based on His majestic character, is not wrapped up in what others think about us.

ଔ If we're not invited to the "cool girl's" night out . . . we are still the daughters of the King.

ଔ If we didn't receive the promotion at work and gain a pay increase . . . we are still loved and cherished by Jesus.

ଔ If Mr. Fabulous dumps us for Ms. Hot Body . . . the King is still enthralled with our beauty.

Through scenario after scenario in our everyday life, what others think of us—or don't think of us—bombards our tender hearts. Our focus often remains on portraying ourselves in the way we want the world to see us, and we make that desired perception our truth. This self-focus is consuming and unproductive because we were not made to focus inward.

Katy Perry's song "Firework" makes my heart smile with its playful beat and uplifting lyrics. The song encourages us to let our personality sparkle and boom while realizing our full potential as a unique human being. The song beats along, reminding us to light our spark to let the whole world see us shine. You should see me jammin' out in my car to this funky pop song. But there is something missing. As I dig into the message behind the message, this song reflects that aspect of self-focus we've discussed in this chapter while leaving out the One who gives us our spark. When we rely on our self rather than focusing on Jesus, insecurities, doubts, and fears threaten the self-made spark that "Firework" talks about. A self-made spark and image is flimsy. It is only when we allow His spark to ignite our true God-given image and personality that we show the world around us our true, authentic selves. It is our raw God-given authenticity that will never fail to attract others.

Our culture tells us we need to elevate ourselves and make our names famous. Broadcasting the inner spark that Katy Perry sings about is easier than ever with a high speed Internet connection and a smartphone. I'm wondering if you would join me in living counter-culturally to the lyrics of songs like "Firework." Philippians 2:9–11 challenges me to resist putting myself out there and, instead, make Jesus famous.

> Therefore God also has highly exalted Him and given Him the name which is above every name, that at the name of Jesus every knee should bow, of those in heaven, and of those on earth, and of those under the earth, and that every tongue should confess that Jesus Christ is Lord, to the glory of God the Father. (Philippians 2:9–11)

We spend so much time focusing on tweaking our image and worrying about the opinions of others that we lose sight of what really matters. What if our image and reputation were entangled in who *He* is instead? Just as our girlfriend Renee mentioned, this would tear Satan up and ruin his plans to keep us fearful of living out the spark that God created in us. When we entangle our sense of self in Him, the pressure to manipulate how people view us is taken away. You and I are then free to immerse ourselves in His Word and soak in His glory. As the Bible states in Philippians chapter 2, one day every single being on the earth will confess and worship Christ as Lord and King. We might as well start focusing our lives outward to reflect His image rather than an inner focus on self!

Journal 4

I FOCUS ON HIM ALONE

Let's take some time to work through the concept of wrapping our self and our focus on the King by looking at a juxtaposition of some thought processes: inner self-focus versus outer focus on the King. First, read the Inner Self-Focus scenario. Then look up the suggested Bible verse to aid you in rewriting the scenario under Outer Focus on the King. Here is an example to get you started:

Inner Self-Focus: Tomorrow I have to give a big presentation at work in which I have to go up against my coworker to pitch an idea, so I'm putting four more hours of work into this already top-notch presentation in order to outshine my competition.

Suggested Verse: "God resists the proud, but gives grace to the humble" (James 4:6).

Outer Focus on the King (scenario rewritten): I've worked so very hard on this project, and I'm confident it will shine. Maybe I can lend a hand to my coworker to see if she needs to practice her pitch?

Your turn . . .

Inner Self-Focus: I don't have anything to offer. Why would that guy ever want to date me?

Suggested Verse: "You shall also be a crown of glory in the hand of the LORD, and a royal diadem in the hand of your God" (Isaiah 62:3).

Outer Focus on the King (scenario rewritten):

_____

_____

_____

_____

Inner Self-Focus: I just can't trust my friends anymore. Once I've been burned, I never forget it. I can't let my heart get close to them again.

Suggested Verse: "Let your conduct be without covetousness; be content with such things as you have. For He Himself has said, 'I will never leave you nor forsake you.' So we may boldly say: 'The Lord is my helper; I will not fear. What can man do to me?'" (Hebrews 13:5–6).

Outer Focus on the King (scenario rewritten):

_____

_____

_____

_____

What other inner self-focus scenarios do you find yourself struggling with? Search the Scripture for some verses that pertain to those situations, and rewrite those scenarios based on His truth.

Stress Diverted

I decided to ask a couple of my 20-something friends how they define the phrase "being comfortable in your own skin" as it relates to self-image. See if you can relate to what they said.

My friend Kristen Lila said: *Being comfortable in your own skin means recognizing your own strengths and talents and using them in the way you were created to. It means not trying to look like, sound like, or be like anyone but yourself. It means embracing your unique quirks, talents, skills, likes, and dislikes.*

Embracing your unique God-given self takes time and attention. Remember what it was like as a teenager when most of our effort was spent trying to look and act like everyone else? Well, as we move into our twenties, that desire to fit in doesn't go away; rather, it changes as we begin to see glimpses of who we want to become. The challenge is to prayerfully dig deeper into our personality, asking God to bring forth our good traits. It takes maturity to ask God to flesh out the junk in our heart that bubbles up in our self-image as well. I love how, in an effort to be the man who completely glorifies God, David literally asked God to search his heart for impurities and flush out the junk.

> Explore me, O God, and know the real me. *Dig deeply and discover who I am.* Put me to the test and watch how I handle the strain. *Examine me* to see if there is an evil bone in me, and guide me down Your path forever. (Psalm 139:23–24 The Voice)

This is certainly not fun, but once we dig through the clutter in our personality, there is more room for the good aspects of our personality to rise and flourish.

My friend Brittany said: *Being comfortable in my own skin means having the peace to walk into a room full of people and not compare my weight, appearance, personality, talents, or accomplishments with anyone else. It means laughing when I want to laugh, saying what I think (with respect and* *kindness, of course), and not second-guessing myself. It doesn't mean that I don't have room for growth or improvement in any of these areas, but that I am only motivated to make changes by God's will and not by the judgment of others. It is my identity in Christ lived out!*

I love how Brittany expresses the forgone need to second guess herself. Maybe you've stayed up at night thinking about something stupid you said in a group conversation and tortured yourself to the point that you've almost e-mailed that group of friends to take back the remark. This business of second-guessing ourselves distracts us from living life in a carefree manner and from saying what we truly mean. I would hate for us to not express ourselves simply because we are worried that our words will come out wrong and people will ostracize us. You, my friend, have so much to offer those in your life. Please don't let your insecurities keep you from feeling comfortable in your own skin.

As you navigate through your twenties, rest assured that everyone else is worried about their image and "who they are." Everyone else is looking within, searching out their passions and their personalities. Because of the simple fact that everyone else is worried about themselves, we can begin to accept who we are, leaving the stress about the opinions of others behind.

Living out the Kingship of Christ in regard to our self-image will take us to a place where we can laugh, sing, speak, work, and relate, all in a manner that jives with our God-given personalities and glorifies our Majestic King. It is easy, though, to slip back into habits of inner self-focus. Take a look at how John the Baptist kept himself in check. In the passage below, John's disciples—the guys he hung out with and ministered with—expressed to John their concern that people were running to Jesus rather than John to be baptized. Though the words John spoke in reply to his disciples were meant to show that the ministry of Jesus was to take precedence over John's work, his statement should permeate our thoughts as well.

51

He [Jesus] must increase, but I must decrease. He who comes from above is above all; he who is of the earth is earthly and speaks of the earth. He who comes from heaven is above all. (John 3:30–32)

A thought process like John's only comes through a true connection with the Majestic King and by approaching the throne in consistent prayer. A humble approach—maybe even physically on our knees—takes us to a place where our self is denied and He is lifted up above all. Where is your heart right now? Focused on self? If so, it's not too late to reverse your course. Take a few moments to journal through some prayer by entering into the throne room and praising Him with a repentant heart that desires to live full of the glory of Jesus.

Journal 5

I LAY IT ALL DOWN BEFORE THE THRONE

Below are some prayer point journal prompts. Finish these thoughts with your own words in a written prayer.

- *Oh Jesus, my Majestic King. Today You have shown me Your glory through Your creation by . . .*

_____

_____

- *Father God, help me to get over myself. I have been self-focused lately in these ways . . .*

_____

_____

- *Thank You, Lord, for searching out my self-focused heart and for cleansing me. I want to focus on You in these ways . . .*

_____

_____

_____

- *May I decrease and You increase in these ways . . .*

_____

_____

_____

*Go to **www.liveitoutblog.com/stress-point** to watch
a video from Sarah on this chapter's Stress Point!*

CHAPTER 3

STRESS POINT:
BODY IMAGE
I HEART THE SKINNY MIRROR

I didn't want to write this chapter. Surely someone else is better equipped to write about body image—someone who no longer struggles with her perception of herself in the mirror. I didn't want to dig deep into my heart to explore why I have such a love/hate relationship with my body. As I converse with my girlfriends about this universal topic, I find there is comfort in the fact that so many of us allow our body image to overtake our life. If you feel as if you are the only one who quietly shudders at the thought of bathing suit shopping or avoids the mirror at all costs, please know that all of us struggle. A few of my girlfriends weighed in on what stresses us out most about our body image:

- *Apparently the twenties are when a woman looks her best. Because of this, I feel like I have this urge to look as good as possible now since it's all downhill from here. I want to have the skinny body complemented by the perfect wavy locks and pretty face.*

- *I'm always stressing about the last ten pounds I need to lose.*

- *I hate my body, and enough people in this world have agreed.*

Body image is an age-old torment of women that is only exacerbated by air-brushed, glossy images in the media of our modern culture. In this chapter we will not dwell on what we cannot change—the media's portrayal of women. Rather, we will look at our own hang-ups and hand them straight to our King, trading the destructive thought processes for daily affirmation that we are His and we are absolutely adored by Him. I have only learned this through hard conversations with the Lord over the years. He's allowed me to suffer through hours of kicking, screaming, and crying over my perception of my body in order to show me how I must yield this stress point to Him.

Because the topic of body image is so very personal to me, I've decided to share my own story for all three girlfriend case studies in this chapter. I hope you don't mind indulging me in this as it is my hope that by sharing the raw and the ugly side of my daily journey to throne of the King, you too will see that we no longer need to live in bondage to ill-conceived perceptions of our body. Friends, we do not have to torture ourselves with this. We don't have to live in the dark spaces of our minds that allow us to think we aren't beautiful enough, skinny enough, fit enough. Join me in my own case studies from different points in my life, and let's look at biblical reasons to love and honor our bodies.

 Girlfriend Case Study #1

Sarah (Me): a high school freshman with an eating disorder. Day after day, I found myself escaping to the bathroom after eating an entire tray of Rice Krispies Treats or after splurging on a Big Mac at lunch. I knew exactly how to hide away to binge and exactly how to stick my finger down my throat, "making things happen" with the least amount of mess. It was an easy fix to my weight problems. I was a cheerleader and shouldered a lot of heavy expectations from those closest to me about how I should look. Of course I had to stay skinny—it was a given. As a typical type A personality who felt the need every single day to control her body, bulimia was the easiest way to take charge. When high school was over, I entered college and began living a more carefree life. I did a lot of soul-searching and healing, and though I would occasionally backslide when my insecurities flamed up with rejections by boyfriends or test papers that reflected poor grades, in time I recovered from bulimia. But the aftermath of my teen years sometimes still lingers. I no longer own a scale. In fact, I refuse to buy one, because back in the day the cold metal box determined my mood for the day. Even now at the doctor's office, I beg the nurse to allow me to close my eyes when I step on the scale and make her swear not to write the number on her chart where I can see it.

 ## Girlfriend Case Study #2

Sarah (Me): a woman with a love for a good fad diet or fitness craze. As I moved through my twenties, the decade brought on a weird love for exercise videos. I loved wasting time watching infomercials selling something that played to the latest fitness craze. I guess it was an escape into a false reality that I too could flaunt a hot, chiseled bod. I flocked toward the videos, and to this day a shelf full of every type of workout DVD (and VHS) takes up space in my house. Oh, I actually did use these videos, but I continued to buy new ones in hopes that the next one would do the trick. And I had to hold onto the old ones in case some new discovery proved that the old method really was the way to go. Crash diets and various cleanses have also taken place over the years, further exacerbating a cycle of wearing a size 10, then 14, then 12 . . . it goes on and on. I'm tired of the agony of my skinny/fat/skinny/fat body cycles. *Why can't I maintain a weight that I'm happy with? What is a weight that I'm happy with, anyway?*

 ## Girlfriend Case Study #3

Sarah (Me): a woman who sometimes feels unavoidably obsessed with her body, even to this day. I know I shouldn't be so obsessed with my body.

Years of loving Jesus has given me head knowledge that I am beautiful in His eyes and that His opinion is the only one that matters. It has taken time for this head knowledge to gravitate toward my heart and become a reality and a life truth. I tend to slip up on my obsessive thoughts during shopping trips and anytime the camera comes out. I know every way to avoid taking pictures of myself and every which way to twist and turn to pose perfectly in hopes that I will look skinnier in the picture. Watching many episodes of *America's Next Top Model* has paid off. When the pictures are printed or posted online, I do one of two things: critique every square inch of the photo of myself or quickly untag myself on Facebook. My friends sure do know how to post pics of themselves that look fantastic, completely disregarding the poor lighting that added an ten extra pounds to *me*. This is where my obsessive brain goes. Some days it's not fun to live in my brain. .

Journal #1

IDENTIFY YOURSELF

• How do you identify with my own girlfriend case studies? Is there one story in particular that rings true for you?

_____

_____

_____

_____

• Let's take a moment to get real and maybe be a little "Debbie Downer." (We will toss away our friend Debbie later in this chapter, don't worry.) Using the space below, list all of your body image issues. Give yourself sixty seconds to do this. Don't dwell on this exercise for longer than that; this is simply a way to flesh out our issues before we go any further.

_____

_____

_____

_____

_____

_____

_____

Worshiping at the Throne of the King

Though I've conquered the behaviors that defined my eating disorder, the thought process behind the disorder creeps in when I'm most vulnerable. As I've learned the importance of daily approaching the throne of the King in worship, I have found that bringing Him my body image is difficult. My body image is one stress point I am most resistant to handing over. About five years ago I spent some time studying biblical worldview—how biblical principles apply to every area of life and culture. It occurred to me that I neglected to see that if promises of Scripture apply to areas of my life like relationships and money, I must not exclude the truths of the Bible with regard to how I view and treat my body.

Interestingly, there is a name for our God that daily reminds me of this. *Elohim* is the name used in reference to our Creator over 2,500 times in the Hebrew Bible. Anytime we see *El* in the Bible, it is referencing God. In this study we have already looked at El Elyon, and we will also look at *El Shaddai* and a few other names of God that start with *El*. The name *Elohim* references God the Father, God the Son (Jesus), and God the Holy Spirit. Three entities of God—all involved in the creation of the universe. Genesis 1:1 says that in the beginning God (*Elohim*) created the heavens and the earth.

In Genesis when God, *Elohim*, flung stars in the sky, raised up mountains from flat land, molded a smoldering sun, hung the moon in the wide abyss of His outer space, and lovingly formed man out of His perfect image, our Creator displayed His creativity in majestic ways not to be outdone. With a heart full of admiration of our King, our Creator, we must not worship the creation—obsess about our body—but rather worship at the glorious throne of the Creator. For when my energy is spent picking and prodding at my self-perceived flaws, I distract my worship from the One who painted my eyes hazel, who tinted my skin a perfect shade of olive, who sculpted my hips with beautiful curves.

Over time, this concept has soaked into the fibers of my brain and it has caused me to rewire my thinking toward Him. I realize now that by concerning myself with my body's imperfections, I'm constantly focused on myself and not on my Creator. This is a subtle form of idolatry that, over time, brings about full-on worship of ourselves rather than our magnificent King. This is not a productive way to spend our precious days here on the earth.

As I've grown closer to my Creator and allowed Him to show me all the ways He thinks I'm beautiful, a hard reality has revealed itself: by treating my body poorly with the bingeing and purging and obsessive thoughts, I was flat out disobeying the very King I so desire to please. When I tear down my body with destructive behavior, I'm defiling His creation.

We wouldn't look up at a rainbow and say, "Hmm . . . that red hue is not quite deep enough." *So why would we look at ourselves (His creation) and criticize our beautiful red hair whose every strand was painted by our Creator with care and craftsmanship?*

We wouldn't look with scorn at a stunningly grand oak tree and mock its extravagant height. *So why would we look in the mirror and throw insults at our beautifully tall stature that our Creator framed just for us?*

We wouldn't kick a cuddly, innocent puppy. *So why would we beat up our own body—the very body that reflects the creativity of our almighty King?*

I love how the first chapters of Genesis give us front-row seats to watch the fantastic dramatics of creation unfold. But as you picture it, don't allow the drama of the creation to dissolve into a cinema-type event that contains no reality. No, this story is more real than any earthly movie producer could ever capture on film. In fact, artists, producers, directors— all modern-day creative professionals—take their cues from our *Elohim* whether they admit it or not. Take a peek with me into the first day of creation.

In the beginning, God created *everything*: the heavens above and the earth *below. Here's what happened: At first* the earth lacked shape and was totally empty, and a dark *fog* draped over the deep while God's spirit-wind hovered over the surface of the *empty* waters. *Then there was the voice of God.*

God: Let there be light.

And light flashed into being. God saw that the light was *beautiful and* good, and He separated the light from the darkness. God named the light "day" and the darkness "night." Evening gave way to morning. That was day one. (Genesis 1:1–5 THE VOICE)

In the very first moments of creation, God formed the earth out of nothing. Who on this earth has the capability to create something out of nothing? No one but our most amazing Creator. As we read through Genesis chapter one, in verse after verse we see God forming the sky, and it was *good*. We see the Creator separate the earth, pour the deep ocean, and it was *good*. We watch Him grow various plants and adorn them with colorful fruits and vegetables, and it was *good*. And then, God formed man—humans—the crown of His creation. With His creative endeavors complete, the Creator "surveyed everything He had made, savoring *its beauty and appreciating its goodness*." (Genesis 1:31 THE VOICE)

Close your eyes and imagine yourself as part of the unfolding drama of creation. Does it warm your heart that your Creator looks at you, savors your beauty, and appreciates the goodness He created in *you*? Let us worship at the throne of our King, where He graces us with His delight in His glorious creation. How can we then criticize, defile, and destruct what our King deems as beautiful and good? How can we disobey the Creator and treat our body in ways that disrespect the craftsmanship that no earthly artist could come close to creating? Take some time at His throne and worship Him, your Creator, by journaling through what you love most about His creation.

Journal 2
I WILL WORSHIP AT THE THRONE OF MY KING

Read Romans 11:36 from *The Voice*:

> For all that exists originates in Him, comes through Him, and is moving toward Him; so give Him the glory forever. Amen.

• Write your name in the blanks as we personalize this verse from Romans.

For _____ exists and originates in Him, _____ comes through Him, and _____ is moving toward Him; so _____ [will] give Him the glory forever. Amen. (Romans 11:36 THE VOICE)

• Do you ever separate yourself out as an exception to God's creation, or do you realize you are special simply because the Creator of the universe savors and appreciates His creation—*you*?

_____

_____

_____

• Write about any difficulties you might have in worshiping the Creator by loving His creation—your body.

_____

_____

_____

- Now for the difficult but very important journal activity. Write out three things you love about your body. If you cannot come up with three, take some time to journal out a prayer asking God to show you what He loves about you, His creation.

Waiting at the Throne of the King

There was a time in my life when I would spend hours on end working out at the gym, and on the days I skipped the gym I would sweat through an aerobic dance video at home. Eventually, my love for working out waned as daily responsibilities piled up and my energy level plummeted. Someone who could once easily complete an advanced salsa dance video with an extra measure of pep soon found herself dreading the idea of an elevated heart rate. It became harder and harder to motivate myself to stay active, and eventually I stopped pushing myself to work out all together.

I could list all of the obvious negative effects that came with my lack of exercise in great detail, among them the fact that my clothes no longer fit. But there were other, more prominent things, too. During the months spent without exercise, I felt lethargic and I constantly craved a nap. I couldn't concentrate at work. My complexion was a mess, my anxiety levels increased, and I suffered back pain due to weak muscles. By letting the responsibilities of life take over my daily calendar, I neglected my responsibility to care for my health.

As women, we often put the needs of others before our own. We also often get caught up in things like logging hours at work as we neglect the benefits of getting in shape. Looking once again at Colossians 3:23, this verse gives me permission to make time for myself in areas like exercise: "Whatever you do, work at it with all your heart, as working for the Lord, not for men" (NIV).

In order to work with all of my heart in my everyday tasks, I must work out with all my heart *physically*. Exercise is a tool I use to keep my body in tune so I can take on life's responsibilities 100 percent. I've also found that exercise improves my body image even before I see improvements in my weight or clothing size. There's something to be said for sweating my hiney off, even if my hiney is not yet smaller. It feels good to get my blood pumping and oxygen flowing, improving my mood and, therefore, my self-image.

Waiting at the throne of our King, our Creator, means we first stop obsessing and idolizing our body. Then and only then will we be able to care for His creation in ·a meaningful way. I found that although I can't spend hours every day in the weight room, it is imperative that I treat my body well by eating healthily, getting a reasonable amount of exercise, and getting plenty of rest. Before you start freaking out thinking your full to-do list won't allow extra time for these things, let me share how I've turned my health around and improved my body image—even when the scale doesn't reflect a big change. Oh wait . . . didn't I say I no longer own a scale? Well, you know what I mean.

- **Carve out a manageable amount of time for exercise**: For me this is thirty minutes, four days a week. But it also means that I have to seriously sweat if I'm only working out for thirty minutes! You might decide you need more than thirty minutes a day, and that is great. Figure out what amount of time reasonably fits into your schedule. Consistency is key in fitness success.

- **Change it up**: Sticking with the same old routine causes boredom and exercise burnout. I like to change it up by playing cardio-heavy Wii games and trying new machines at the gym.

- **Be realistic**: Keep yourself motivated by simply giving yourself a break. If you miss a day of exercise, try not to obsess over the missed opportunity to burn calories. Instead, appreciate your body's need to recover, then get back out there and sweat after a good day's rest.

- **Place food in its rightful place**: I pack healthy snacks like fruit, nuts, cereal and tons of water bottles in my little lunch bag to eat and drink throughout the day. This helps me from stopping at McDonalds for an easy drive-through lunch.

- **Sleep, Girlfriend!**: Oh how I love my naps. I also shoot for eight hours of sleep every night. When I don't sleep, the exhaustion causes me to let my guard down and slip back into unhealthy eating habits. I'm also too fatigued to work out. To make sure I'm getting enough sleep, I'm intentional about signing off social media and e-mail, turning off the television (this is when DVR comes in handy), and making myself get rest, knowing the benefits of sleep outweigh those of catching up on my shows.

(Be sure to check out the appendix in the back of this book for other resources from health and fitness experts to encourage you to achieving better health and a better body image.)

I'm still on the journey back to fitness, and I won't pretend that it has been easy. In the past several months, I've learned that I love feeling energetic and focused as I do life to the best of my ability for the Lord. Oh, and the good night's sleep after a kickin' workout doesn't hurt either! Rather than checking the box and just doing life on auto-drive, I've slowed down and worked on intentionally approaching my body and health in a way that would make Jesus, my Creator, smile.

A good friend of mine whom I look to as my fitness guru recently posted something on her blog that confirmed what the Lord is teaching me about my body. Michelle Myers wrote some of the most life-giving words that any woman who struggles with her body and weight could read. She wrote, "So, how can you discover your happy weight? There are two key factors: Your happy weight is what your body will naturally reach when you are eating healthy and exercising regularly. So don't get hung up on the scale or what number you wish was written on the tag of your jeans. Continuously make healthy decisions, and results will follow."[5]

We must continuously make these decisions by approaching the throne of our Creator daily, and some days hourly and minute by minute. When I want to slack off from my workout for the day, I wait at the throne by recognizing that the decision to sweat and take care of my body pleases Him. When I just can't pass up a Big Mac and fries, I wait at the throne of my Creator asking Him to help me make wise eating decisions for the remainder of the day. Let us wait at the throne with every little temptation to disrespect our body and trade in those temptations with actions that lift up His creation—our body.

Journal 3
I WILL WAIT AT THE THRONE OF MY KING

- Revisit Colossians 3:23 (mentioned on page 65) as it relates to physically taking care of your body in order to work with all your heart in your job, your life, etc. What are your thoughts on this concept?

- List some specific ways you can better care for the King's creation—your body. (For example: rest, exercise, healthy eating)

- Sometimes it is scary to make changes in our lives; even changes that make us take a good hard look at our bodies. Soak in these words from Hebrews:

    Let us then fearlessly and confidently and boldly draw near to the throne of grace (the throne of God's unmerited favor to us sinners), that we may receive mercy [for our failures] and find grace to help in good time for every need [appropriate help and well-timed help, coming just when we need it]. (Hebrews 4:16 AMPLIFIED BIBLE)

Let's break down this verse as it pertains to our need to care for our bodies.

• How can you fearlessly and confidently and boldly draw near to the throne with your body image issues?

_____

_____

_____

• Do you see that these heartfelt needs regarding your body image are important to your King?

_____

_____

_____

• What kind of mercy and grace (forgiveness and help) do you need when you approach the throne of the King, your Creator?

_____

_____

_____

_____

Finding Focus on Him Alone

THE SKINNY MIRROR

You all know what I'm talking about: the skinny mirror, and the not-so-skinny mirror. Some clothing retailers get this dressing room nuance completely right, and some just don't. And you know exactly what I mean, don't you? Those mirrors whose tilt makes you look instantly slim can boost your self-esteem, whereas the ones whose tilt is a bit off can make you feel like you might as well drown your sorrows in a pack of Oreos, like, right now! Isn't it crazy how a certain tilt of the mirrored glass and the precise angle of the lighting fixture can either make a shopping experience glorious or disastrous?

On a recent shopping trip with a friend, I encountered the not-so-skinny mirror. Those darling jeans clung to the wrong curves. That chic tank top did nothing for my figure. The bathing suit was just not cute. Within a matter of minutes the thrill of the bargain buy dissolved into a tailspin of self-critique. My mind was consumed with how I looked as I allowed the not-so-skinny mirror to determine my mood for the rest of the afternoon.

But before I infected my shopping partner with my self-pity, I felt the Lord say in my heart something I have not forgotten since my ill-fated run-in with that horrible mirror. He said, *Sarah, your beauty and worth are not determined by what you see in a mirror. Take your focus off of yourself and find focus on Me.*

Find *focus on Him*. A sense of relief came over me as I inhaled and exhaled those words. These three words have become my battle cry when I face both the not-so-skinny mirror and the skinny mirror. Anytime I am more consumed with myself than I am with God, I end up focusing on everything that is wrong in my life. On the flip side, anytime that I am more consumed with God than I am with myself, I am better equipped to walk out of that dressing room with the understanding that I am okay. I recount the ways He thinks I am beautiful; I'm reminded that I am His creation and He finds me special. On days that the mirror is kind to me and I actually feel beautiful, I wonder how my perspective would change if I took a moment to give thanks to my Creator for giving me a beautiful body, curves and all. Giving thanks redirects my attitude on skinny-mirror days as well as not-so-skinny-mirror days.

So, when I find focus on Him I am able to get over myself.

It's a simple yet complicated truth, but one worth playing over and over in my mind. In order to get over myself, I must quit obsessing over things like the way I look in pictures, how a certain pair of pants fit, or the fact that there's a big zit on my chin. After all, this time spent in the space of my mind is not productive whatsoever. When I let ugly thoughts about God's creation swirl around and twist into non-realities, I'm living in a place in my mind that purely focuses on the creation and not the Creator. I begin to worship the creation, and I forget the reality that God is more worthy of my worship than I am. The book of Romans tackles the idea of sins of the flesh—anything that takes our focus off of Jesus and separates us from Him in our disobedience to the words in the Bible. When we obsess over our literal *flesh*—how we look in the mirror or the number on the tag in our new jeans—this is no less a sin than lying or cheating.

> If you live your life animated by the flesh—*namely, your fallen, corrupt nature*—then your mind is focused on the matters of the flesh. But if you live your life animated by the Spirit—*namely, God's indwelling presence*—then your focus is on the work of the Spirit. A mind focused on the flesh is doomed to death, but a mind focused on the Spirit will find full life and complete peace. (Romans 8:5–6 THE VOICE)

When we focus on our body image junk, thought by thought we step away from our Creator's perfect peace. Something happens to me when I obsess over my body: my entire life turns dark, and nothing is right in my world. The obsession bleeds into other parts of my life, and I resent that I'm not happy about my body and therefore am not happy in my job, with my family, with my friends. But blessings are offered by our King to a mind that turns outward toward Him rather than inward toward our perceived flaws. God's beautiful bounty consists of contentment, joy, fun, and relief.

Again, we must get over ourselves and make much of Him. With a heart of thanksgiving, we celebrate aspects of our bodies like good health. We praise Him that we have able bodies to do the work that He set out for us to do before time began.

> For we are the product of His hand, *heaven's poetry etched on lives*, created in the Anointed, Jesus, to accomplish the good works God arranged long ago. (Ephesians 2:10 The Voice)

We can't fulfill the heavenly plans of our King if we mistreat our bodies, whether physically or in our thoughts. How can we love others if we don't love ourselves as Jesus loves us? How do we serve others from a heart that's depleted and self-defeated? How do we volunteer our time and talent if our energy level is low because we didn't nurture our body? These noble acts that glorify God are only accomplished when we turn our focus away from that skinny or not-so-skinny mirror and direct it instead on pleasing and serving the Lord. I don't know about you, but I sure don't want to miss out on the blessing of pouring myself out for someone else and therefore worshiping Jesus. Let us stop right this moment with the torturous thought processes that tear down the creation and make a pact to . . .

Get over ourselves.

Journal 4
I FIND FOCUS ON HIM ALONE

• Does the phrase "get over yourself" sound harsh to you? If so, why? If not, how does it help you to redirect your focus back to the Creator?

• Read through Ephesians 2:10 (mentioned on page 72) several times. What are some ways that you have allowed your body image issues to overtake your attitude toward life in general and keep you from living out what great plans God has for you?

• How can you hand those issues straight over to Jesus? What benefits do you see in allowing your focus to turn back to the Creator rather than on how you see yourself in the mirror?

Stress Diverted

My prayer is that you, my sweet friend, will see yourself as a precious jewel that sparkles and shines in the heavenly throne room that is the perspective of our almighty King, the Ultimate Creator. Though we were once trapped in the filth of our sin and in a true state of disarray both inwardly and outwardly, we no longer live in the muck when we accept that Jesus is King of Kings and Lord of lords. This very King saved us from the depths of evil sin initiated by Satan and continued in the garden of Eden when Adam and Eve covered their bodies in shame. You and I are not required to hide and cover our bodies in embarrassment. Let us adorn ourselves in the beauty that outshines any length of time or amount of wear this earth has to throw at us.

One of my girlfriends once said of her body that it "all goes downhill" after your twenties. I chuckled a bit at the statement, because I, too, have seen the effects of time and gravity on my body post-twenties. But with time and a real effort to care for the creation—the very body that God sculpted by hand—I've come to a sense of peace and gratitude. Some days, admittedly, it's hard to feel that gratitude and peace when I just want to wallow in pity over the lumps and bumps and lines of my body. But what the Lord has shown me and what I hope to show you, too, is that . . .

> even if we spend hours at the gym squatting and butt lifting, none of those repetitions count if the Lord is not lifted high in our life;
>
> even if we polish our skin, ridding it of zits, lines, or cellulite, we will never buff out the everlasting love that Jesus has for our hearts, not for our perfect complexions; and
>
> none of our sweat equity and calorie burning counts if we've wasted our day on serving ourselves rather than loving and serving others.

The world may look at us and place value on our lives based on our bra size, our waist size, and the number on the scale, but we simply do not have to follow suit. Let's not allow those values to rule our lives, especially when the Word of our King tells us that "Charm is deceitful and beauty is passing, but a woman who fears the LORD, she shall be praised" (Prov. 31:30).

Journal 5
I LAY IT ALL DOWN BEFORE THE THRONE

- Father God, my amazing Creator, show me the ways You think I am beautiful . . .

_____

_____

- Lord, I want to believe that You value and love me based on my heart and not my body. I give my body issues over to You . . .

_____

_____

- Lord, forgive me when I obsess over my body image in these ways . . .

_____

_____

- Thank You, Lord for these attributes of myself that I know You crafted with such detail and care . . .

_____

_____

*Go to **www.liveitoutblog.com/stress-point** to watch
a video from Sarah on this chapter's Stress Point!*

CHAPTER 4

STRESS POINT:
LOVE/DATING
PART 1
HE *IS* JUST THAT
INTO YOU

Most of us have experienced the excruciating pain of dating. You might not recognize just how difficult it's been until you consider it in retrospect, after you've found that special relationship that rocks your world, but the stress of finding the perfect guy is continuously on the minds of many women in their twenties. Please know that you aren't alone in your quest to find love and that your anxieties in this area aren't unusual. Find comfort in the fact that the mistakes you make are most likely being repeated by women all over the world. It's a cutthroat arena in which it's all too easy to lose track of your identity and your purity. The women in this chapter's case studies represent your personal life; they're your girlfriends who are struggling alongside you right now with the dating scene. Take a glimpse inside their lives and their mistakes, and then see how the Lord in His perfect timing has turned their situations around, placing each of them in a positive relationship with a man who finds them lovely and worthwhile.

Girlfriend Case Study #1

Gigi from the movie *He's Just Not That into You.* On the surface it seems as though Gigi has her life in order—good job, great friends, and a fun single life in Baltimore. Yet she continues to strike out in the dating realm. Gigi is nothing short of obsessed when she actually finds a guy who shows a bit of interest in her. In one hilarious scene, she stresses about a phone call to someone she has recently met at a bar. After spending a long while preparing for the phone conversation by scribbling a practice "dialogue," Gigi dials the guy's number with paper and pen in hand, only to end up reaching his voicemail. We then see her stumbling ridiculously over what to say and completely botching the message. Gigi has let herself become consumed with dating to the point that her enthusiastic approach drives potential boyfriends away. At the heart of it, Gigi longs to be loved, romanced, and told that she's special and beautiful. But the route she takes toward this goal is bumpy.

 ## Girlfriend Case Study #2

Allison: a darling young entrepreneur in a small town where the single male population is lacking, both in quantity and quality. Allison has spent two years of her life with a guy who isn't cutting it in terms of his boyfriend duties. She is constantly in a state of "Where is this thing going?" This beautiful, fit, intelligent woman who loves the Lord could have spent these past years looking for a man who cherishes her, yet something has kept her coming back to this guy who takes her for granted. In a recent e-mail Allison laid out several things she wants from this man, none of which is too far off base or too much to ask:

1. Call me your girlfriend and be proud that you're with me.

2. Bring me around your family and make me feel special.

3. Let me go to church with you.

Her boyfriend thought these three important requests were too much to ask, so Allison finally realized she had to cut ties with him, yet she still can't totally break away.

 ## Girlfriend Case Study #3

Rachel: a young executive in a big city with a boyfriend who won't commit. Rachel fell in love when her boyfriend swept her off her feet after she had experienced a devastating personal loss and her vulnerability led to a need for security. The two dated for several years and ended up living in a house together that he bought and she decorated. Rachel so desperately wanted to make this house her home. Several years had gone by when Rachel began to express her strong desire to be married and have children. Her boyfriend would agree verbally but continuously put her off because the messy end to a past relationship had devastated him, leaving him afraid to commit. This upset Rachel, who knew he had commitment issues but had stayed with him in the hope that he would one day come around. But in the end she realized she had spent the better portion of her twenties pining away for marriage and children with a man who might not ever give her those things.

Journal 1

IDENTIFY YOURSELF

- With which of the girlfriends in this chapter's case studies do you most identify? Why?

_____

_____

_____

- What is it about her dating situation that is similar to your own?

_____

_____

_____

- In what ways does dating stress you out?

_____

_____

_____

- Describe your ideal guy (how he treats you, how you relate to each other, what you have in common, his personality, his relationship with the Lord, etc.).

_____

_____

_____

_____

Worshiping at the Throne of the King

Dating is not fun—or at least it isn't all fun. Once you get past the excitement of the moment you meet and the thrill of that first phone call when he asks you out, dating can be treacherous. I'm sure Gigi loved the thrill of the chase, yet she rushed her relationships and inadvertently annoyed her potential suitors. Most women, like Gigi, do enjoy the thrill of the chase in dating. But on the flip side, women are fashioned by God to be the object of the chase. Let me explain via a quote from *He's Just Not That into You*:

> A man who wants to make a relationship work will move mountains to keep the woman he loves. If he's not calling you to tell you he loves you and wants you back, it should only be because he's showing up at your new residence to do it in person . . . if he's not doing any of that, he may love you, he may miss you, but ultimately he's just not that into you. Stop taking his calls and let him know what it's like to live without you.

In their book *Captivating*, John and Staci Eldredge take a hard look at the souls of women and describe romance in a way that speaks directly to the heart:

> God is the author of romance. It is his idea and he is the best at it. It is wonderful to be in a loving relationship with a man, to share life, to have romance and intimacy in tangible ways. . . . No matter how much a man pours into our hearts, we still long for more. . . . Only God can meet it [the longing for romance] in the deepest and most substantive, life changing way.[6]

This author of romance is our Immanuel, God with us. We see the name Immanuel used in the New Testament when God announces to Mary, Jesus' mother, that she will give birth to a son and they will call Him Immanuel, God with us (Matthew 1:22–24). You might recall this detail from the Christmas story; I know the sweetness of the idea that God is *with* us has stuck with me since childhood. God literally came to earth to be with us when He sent His Son, Jesus. Then, because Jesus, our

81

Immanuel, died on the cross for us, we still have God *with* us as the Holy Spirit living in our heart. All it takes to feel God's presence with you is to believe that Jesus is your Lord, Savior, and King.

Through every stage of life—the good, the bad, and the ugly—God is with us. This includes our romantic life. What girl doesn't want to feel as though she's the only one in the room, the most beautiful, absolutely captivating to someone? Our Immanuel makes this a reality. The people of God, the Israelites, lived in an on-again, off-again relationship with God in which they continuously fell away from and cycled back to their belief in their Immanuel. We too often live out this type of faith, as dating is usually a distraction to our all-out worship at the throne of our King. Yet He continues to welcome us back, forgiving our waywardness. Does the following verse rock your socks off, or what?

> You shall be a crown of beauty in the hand of the LORD, and a royal diadem in the hand of your God. You shall no more be termed Forsaken, and your land shall no more be termed Desolate, but you shall be called My Delight Is In Her. (Isaiah 62:3–4 ESV)

Can you imagine yourself as someone's delight—his one and only? Since this image is so much more fulfilling than worshiping the act of dating, allow this declaration to soak into your mind and heart: God, *your Immanuel*, is *your* ultimate Romancer. As you worship the One who crowns you with His love, measure each potential boyfriend or husband against the standard Immanuel sets before you.

Immanuel also mends our heart from past hurt. If you're experiencing the trials of a breakup, heartache, or uncertainty about where you stand in a particular relationship, let this verse from Hosea warm your soul:

> Therefore, behold, I will allure her, and bring her into the wilderness, and speak tenderly to her. (Hosea 2:14 ESV)

The Lord brings us out of a dry wilderness and refreshes our hearts with deep drafts of His living water. Never forget that our God may allow the time we spend dating to feel like time in the wilderness. When we're thirsty for the Lord, we race through the hot sands of the desert to the cool shade where He stands with open arms, waiting to accept us and quench our yearning. God wants us to long for Him, and Him alone. He calls us to worship at His throne because this worship puts us in a mind-set in which He alone can meet our needs and speak to our hearts. Because He is Immanuel, God with Us, the Lord knows our desires in dating, and He truly does want us to find happiness and love—the kind only He can give. When we are secure in worshiping at the throne of our Immanuel, our God who is always with us no matter what, we are okay with even being without a boyfriend or husband. At first the concept might be scary, but He pours His love and security over us and we grow to be okay with whatever romantic situation we find ourselves in.

Journal 2
I WILL WORSHIP AT THE THRONE OF MY KING

Read Zephaniah 3:17:

> The LORD your God in your midst, the Mighty One, will save; He will rejoice over you with gladness, He will quiet you with His love, He will rejoice over you with singing.

• Let's make this personal. Fill in your name in each of the blanks.

The LORD your God is in _____'s midst, the Mighty One, will save; He will rejoice over _____ with gladness, He will quiet _____ with His love, He will rejoice over _____ with singing.

• Based on the passage above, write down in your own words the ways in which God will interact with you.

_____

_____

_____

_____

_____

• Have you longed for this deep, passionate type love from a guy and come up short? Most likely all of us have or will in the future. Even if you've found your "Prince Charming," he'll never measure up to the Lord in terms of demonstrating his love. How does this reality speak to you right now, in your present dating situation? If you are not in a dating relationship, how does this verse encourage you and show you the deep love that Jesus has for *you*?

_____

_____

_____

_____

_____

- It might be hard to grasp this type of relationship with God. Do you have a hard time "allowing" the Lord to be delighted in you? Do you feel worthy of having Him rejoice over you?

_____

_____

_____

_____

- Please know that you *are* worthy of being delighted in, rejoiced over, and covered in His love. Take a moment to let that sink in; then write out what you're feeling.

_____

_____

_____

_____

_____

Waiting at the Throne of the King

You've probably heard the phrase "Why buy the cow when you can get the milk for free?" I continuously remind my friends of this adage in the midst of their turmoil with their noncommittal boyfriends, as they give away their hearts and bodies to men who are unwilling to reciprocate in their intensity and love. So many women jump into bed with their boyfriends, only to end up haunted by emptiness and dissatisfaction. Many believe that every sexual relationship leaves a permanent imprint on our heart and mind. Wouldn't we hate to taint a beautiful and pure sexual relationship with our future husband by drudging up thoughts of sexual forays with past boyfriends? I'm in no way pointing fingers; I'll be the first to admit my mistakes in the area of sex. But as your older girlfriend, I hope to convey some truth on this subject, even if I've learned these lessons the hard way.

Waiting at the throne of our King, Immanuel, includes saving sex for marriage. Intimacy with our future husband is God's ultimate plan for us as His created daughters. This concept is extremely countercultural, something even women who grow up in church find hard to swallow. Our culture claims that this philosophy is old-fashioned and unnecessary. But I would venture to say that movies like *He's Just Not That into You* wouldn't even come out had the world embraced the concept of abstinence until marriage. As I watched this movie, I cringed in acknowledgment of my ready empathy toward the characters, especially because the writers were so clearly influenced by real-life women struggling to find true, meaningful love. It's hard to watch characters like Gigi, since I've stood in her cute little high-heeled shoes. The games played in the dating realm can be pure torture.

The way to survive in the dating world is to find ourselves at the throne of the King, seeking His guidance and sweet romance. I encourage you to make time daily to speak to God about your current dating situation. Seek His Word to know how you should proceed with the man you are seeing.

Below are a few important questions to cover with the Lord. Be honest with Him in your feelings and emotions.

ন্ত Does He [God] approve of the man you are dating?

ন্ত Does He condone your behavior with this guy?

ন্ত Does this guy love Jesus?

If you can honestly answer yes to the questions above, the man you're dating will respect you enough to put a ring on your finger before you become intimate in the bedroom. As much as he might want to give in to your mutual sexual urges, this man will acknowledge that waiting is God's plan for marriage and sex, and he will hold fast to the commands of the Lord. Let your Immanuel take care of the matchmaking, and attune yourself to His guidance and direction while dating.

Our case study girlfriend Rachel finally left her boyfriend and moved out of town for a fresh start. I believe the Lord has spoken to her about her past relationship and is healing her tender heart. It's not easy to continue to live with integrity and purity while dating in this fast-paced, sex-crazed world. We'll probably field questions from our friends, such as "How can you really know he's the one until you sleep with him?" They don't get it, and it might be tempting to give in and go with the flow. If this is your temptation, hold fast to the fact that the Lord is captivated by you. What a clear example of how a man should see you if he's meant to be your lifelong mate.

Journal 3

I WAIT AT THE THRONE OF MY KING

Imitating God includes reading the Bible and actually doing what God commands of us. Based on the following passage in Ephesians, God warns us not to partake in sexual promiscuity:

> Watch what God does, and then you do it, like children who learn proper behavior from their parents. Mostly what God does is love you. . . . Love like that. Don't allow love to turn into lust, setting off a downhill slide into sexual promiscuity. (Ephesians 5:1–3 MSG)

• Journal through your experience with sex and relationships. Have you experienced times when you've slipped downhill into sexual promiscuity? Take some time to be honest with the Lord about where you've slipped, and allow Him to forgive you and heal your heart.

• Earlier in this chapter, I posed some questions to think about when evaluating your present dating relationship. Further explore your thoughts and answers to the questions. If you aren't in a relationship, journal through how you imagine those questions would be answered if or when the time comes. This is important to file away for the future. I wish I had evaluated my hopeful answers ahead of time!

Finding Focus in Him Alone

Jesus is explicit regarding what He expects of us and where our daily, moment-by-moment focus should be. When asked about His greatest commandment, Jesus replied: "You shall love the LORD your God with all your heart, with all your soul, and with all your mind" (Matthew 22:37).

This applies as much to dating as to every other facet of our lives. Every issue we encounter with regard to the opposite sex should be bounced off these questions:

Do I still love my God with my whole heart, soul, and mind?

Is my potential boyfriend doing the same?

By using this standard as our barometer for future activities with men, we'll not only please the Lord but prevent untold heartache as well. When we focus on Him, our priorities in dating will align themselves without a struggle.

When we train our focus on God and His Word in this area, we also come to recognize traits the Bible lays out for how a husband should love his wife. The Bible is unequivocal on this issue. Although its guidelines don't pertain to the dating relationship per se, we do receive from its pages clear guidance on what we should be able to expect from our godly boyfriends. If there's one phrase to which I return again and again when talking to my girlfriends, it's this: *Don't settle for less.*

For a long time, both Rachel and Allison stuck with status quo in their relationships—and lived miserably. They accepted their boyfriends' non-committal attitudes and pressed on in hope that their men might change.

When we're in a continual state of communication with Jesus, we know in our hearts that this behavior on the part of the men in our lives doesn't cut it and that it's time for us to move on. But if we're out of tune with the Lord's guidance, we may well have no clue that a relationship of this quality isn't what God has planned for our lives. If we want to move from a troubled relationship to one that both thrills and fulfills us, we need to take the first step of allowing the Lord to lead us.

Finding our focus in the Lord alone helps us see that we don't have to obsess over a troubled relationship. Allison lives in constant anxiety, continuously second-guessing her own merit and asking why this guy doesn't treat her the way she deserves to be treated—the way God wants and designed her to be treated. The Great Commandment that teaches us to love our God with all our hearts implies the importance of focusing our worship and our waiting on Him first, before anyone or anything else. This is tough to do when our thought patterns cycle continuously around futile questions like *When will he call? Why am I not number one in his life? Does he really love me?*

However, these questions are answered by God, about God, and cut straight to the heart of your anxieties. The Lord really does love you; why else would He have sent Jesus to the cross specifically for you? God calls your name each day in His yearning to draw you near to Himself and heal your wounds. No matter how anxious you might be over where you stand with that guy, you can rest in God, assured that you're numero uno in the heart of your Immanuel.

Journal 4
I FOCUS IN HIM ALONE

Let's take another look at Ephesians 5, this time focusing on verse 2.

> Keep company with him and learn a life of love. Observe how Christ loved us. His love was not cautious but extravagant. He didn't love in order to get something from us but to give everything of himself to us. (Ephesians 5:2 MSG)

• The only way to live a "life of love" is to continually focus our attention on Jesus and His example of love. Once our focus is on Him, we can imitate how He loves and show our boyfriends that kind of love. How can you, today, turn your attention and affection back toward Jesus?

• What would it mean for you to be loved in the way you need? What actions or words speak love to you? If you have a boyfriend right now, does he love you in this way? If you are between relationships, have past boyfriends loved you in this way?

• Notice the word *extravagant* in Ephesians 5:2. Define it in your own words. Is it difficult to love extravagantly? Why or why not?

Stress Diverted

The Lord will continue nudging us toward necessary course co..
along our relationship paths as long as we worship, wait, and focus on Him.
We're guaranteed a less stressful romantic life when we don't command
the same love and security from a man that our Immanuel offers us daily.
No human being will ever match in lavishness the love God pours into our
hearts so freely. Many women rely on a man to fill their void, or "cup."
When he doesn't live up to their expectations, they revert to a state of
despair and loneliness. But there's good news: God can and will fill our cup
to the point of overflowing. At that point, anything our boyfriends can add
to that cup is simply a blessing, kind of like icing on the cake. (We will go
into greater detail about allowing the Lord to "fill our cups" in chapter 5.)

This realization on the part of you and your boyfriend takes the burden off the godly man, freeing him up to be himself and to discover, along
with you, why God loves us so much. God will never leave you hanging
and uncertain, confused and frustrated. For a time you might find yourself
without a boyfriend, but such an interval of waiting only serves to prepare
you for that relationship that will glorify Him and align with His principles.
There's no need to live in constant stress over love and dating. Cast all
your anxieties on God, trusting that He is enthralled with your beauty and
wants only the best for you.

When you bring your dating stress point to the Lord, He stands ready
to speak encouragement into your heart—if you'll stop long enough to
listen. Here's a sample prayer for times when your heart is aching or you're
tempted to give in:

> *My Lord, my God who is always with me, You are captivated by my*
> *beauty. I trust You to lead me into a relationship with a man who is in*
> *love with me just the way You are. I wait for You and Your guidance.*

Whether or not you're in a relationship, another productive way to
spend your time waiting and worshiping is to pray for your future spouse.

The guy you're dating may or may not fit that role, so go ahead and pray more generally for the one God has planned for you. This might seem crazy, since you have no idea who he is or where he may be, but what if this man is going through a difficult time, and your prayers will make all the difference in the world? What if he, too, doubts his direction in finding a life partner, and your prayers lead him to find comfort and strength in the Lord? What if he finds himself in the midst of temptation that will lead him, without your intervention, toward having sex with another woman? Your prayers could help direct God's wisdom and commandments straight to his heart, causing him to refrain from taking that step. Prayer—whether our own or others' on our behalf—is a powerful tool that brings us closer to God and prevents us from making mistakes we would regret once we are married.

Please know that I feel your pain of frustration and uncertainty. Endless questions may be swirling through your head and invading your heart: *Will God ever put a man in my life who loves and cherishes me? Aren't I good enough? Or pretty enough?* Don't let such doubts deflect your focus from your Immanuel. Even though your close friend just got engaged, or your coworker just received a showy bouquet of roses, cling ever so tightly your Immanuel who is always with you in the turmoil of dating. When you grip the hand of Jesus and position yourself permanently at His throne, you'll grow in ways that won't cease to surprise you. This increased maturity prepares each one of us for the relationship that will rock our world. This relationship can only come when we weigh all of our thoughts and decisions against what the Bible has to say about love. I encourage you to worship, wait, and focus on your Immanuel with the expectation that what He has planned for you will exceed your wildest dreams. Even if His plans for you are not to marry, your Immanuel has your life planned out to the utmost perfection that will add up to greatness no matter what. He promises us that, regardless of our romantic relationships, or lack thereof, all things work together for good for those who love, seek, and cherish their Immanuel (Romans 8:28).

Journal 5
I LAY IT ALL DOWN BEFORE THE THRONE

Below are some prayer point journal prompts. Finish these thoughts with your own words in a written prayer.

• *My Lord, Immanuel, I thank You for Your extravagant love. Lately, You have shown me Your love in these ways . . .*

_____

_____

• *Father, I've been hurt in past dating relationships. I hand over to You these hurts right now so that You can enable and equip me to move forward . . .*

_____

_____

• *Show me how to love You extravagantly. Then show me how to love others in the same way . . .*

_____

_____

• *Father, forgive me for not having waited to be intimate with my boyfriend. I accept Your forgiveness and ask for strength to wait in the future . . .*

_____

_____

*Go to **www.liveitoutblog.com/stress-point** to watch
a video from Sarah on this chapter's Stress Point!*

CHAPTER 5

STRESS POINT:
LOVE/DATING
PART 2
QUITE INTENSE

In the last chapter we started a discussion on dating and found ourselves at the throne of our King even amidst the flurry of emotions and uncertainty that often bubbles up as we encounter this stress point. We looked at relationships in which the guy wouldn't commit after long-term dating, and we explored situations where we have to come to grips with the fact that he just might not be into us. In this chapter let's talk about when dating relationships move into the arena of potential engagement and marriage— when things intensify. This is not the time to live out casual worship of the Lord. Instead, when our relationships move to the next level it is crucial to cement our feet at His throne, keeping us from the well-known cliché of being totally swept off our feet in passion and romantic love. Our hearts swell and our face is plastered with an unfaltering grin as we dream about a white dress, a handsome groom, a wedding cake, sparkly diamonds, and a honeymoon on a secluded island. These things quickly pull our focus off of Jesus and put us at risk of losing sight of what is important: loving Him and allowing Him to be our ultimate Romancer, thus keeping us grounded and able to love and serve our soon-to-be husband well.

If you are presently single or without a serious boyfriend, please don't skip this chapter. I hope that you will tuck away for the future the truths in the next few pages. It is always a good thing to have your priorities figured out before diving into any type of relationship.

Our next three girlfriend case studies take us through three stages of an intense, committed relationship. I call the stages pre-intensity, present-intensity, and sustained-intensity. You will come to know these stages well as we work through this chapter.

Girlfriend Case Study #1
(PRE-INTENSITY STAGE)

Avery: a college freshman who moved several states away from home to attend her dream college. Avery was excited to get a business marketing degree, but being a sweet romantic at heart, she also looked forward to finding her future husband somewhere, sometime during the next four years. Avery was different from her college suite-mates in that she had a level of love and worship of Jesus that most eighteen-year-old girls lack. She committed a true, affectionate heart to her Lord and King even in the arena of dating. Several weeks into her first semester, Avery received a clear prompt from the Lord that she was not to date anyone during her freshman year. Disappointment kept her mad at God for a few days, and Avery told Him as much. But, because she knew in her heart that obedience is the best option, Avery settled into the idea that this freshman year just might be a little lonely. Much to her delight, though, the nights when Avery's friends were dressing up to go out on dates, the Lord filled her heart with pure worship and peace in Him, making the dateless freshman year satisfying nonetheless.

Girlfriend Case Study #2
(PRESENT-INTENSITY STAGE)

Shelby: a beautiful twenty-three-year-old waitress working on her gradu-ate degree who has waited her entire twenties to find "the one." After several relationships in which Shelby ended up with a hurt heart, the Lord wrapped her wounds with a promise that, one day in the future, He had a man planned for her who would make the pain from the past jerks worth-while. Many years later at age twenty-nine, God came through with His promise and dropped Shelby's future husband into her life, jump-starting a whirlwind engagement. Six months before their sweet, simple, elegant wedding day, Shelby and her fiancé set out to draw boundaries and set measures of accountability in order to keep their relationship pure. Both determined that the excitement of the upcoming wedding as well as the chemistry between them wouldn't come between the commitments they both separately made to God in years past: that He would always be first and foremost no matter the fire and passion of a newly intensified relationship.

Girlfriend Case Study #3
(SUSTAINED-INTENSITY STAGE)

Sarah (Me): a not-so-newlywed who has been married to her husband, Greg, for ten years. When Greg and I met, fell in love, and got married, I was the one in our relationship with a "past," but as the years ticked by, my guilt about being the one who had dated around waned. I found absolute forgiveness from the Lord, and Greg never thought twice about my past. One thing that continued through the years, though, was this perception of Greg that I carried. I assumed that because he didn't make the mistakes I made in college, he was pure and perfect. From the onset of our relationship, I set Greg up on a pedestal. Four years into our marriage, God knocked Greg off the pedestal I placed him on and helped me to see that Greg was not the picture of absolute perfection. A mistake that Greg admitted to socked me in the gut, and the reality set in that my husband was an imperfect human just like me. This mistake was not a fatal blow to our marriage or anything, but it did impact, for the good, my view of Greg, though he never stopped being sweet, loving, kind, handsome, and incredibly faithful to me.

Journal 1
IDENTIFY YOURSELF

- What is your relationship status right now?

  _____

  _____

  _____

- In addition to the obvious goal of engagement and marriage, what is your personal definition of an intense relationship?

  _____

  _____

  _____

  _____

- List a few concerns or questions you might have regarding the preparation for an intense relationship. What areas of your heart and affections do you need to take to the throne of the King when you think about engagement and marriage? If you are presently not in an intense relationship, journal through your perceptions of this stage of life.

  _____

  _____

  _____

  _____

  _____

  _____

Worshiping at the Throne of the King
(Pre-Intensity Stage)

What I love about Avery is her sold out heart for Jesus; she truly delights herself in the Lord and immerses herself in His presence daily by soaking in the Bible and praying, even through life's trivial moments. When I first met Avery, her absolute abandon for the Lord astonished me in its contrast to our culture's view of self, sex, and materialism. I have to admit that Avery's love for her King challenges me and makes me want to love Jesus like she does: to consume my life with what pleases Him, to fill my day with conversation and continual connection at the throne of my King.

Whether or not we live out our faith like Avery does, the Lord desires and even requires from us a commitment to Him to put aside all worldly things—including our intense romantic relationships—and to hand over our hearts to Him in all-out worship. You and I serve a jealous God. The word *jealous* comes up forty times in the Old Testament. The Lord revealed Himself to the Israelites as a Divine, Jealous God after He brought Israel out of slavery in Egypt and provided for their every need while traveling in the desert. Yet the Israelites created gold statues (idols) that they worshiped instead of God, and this infuriated Him.

> For the LORD your God is a consuming fire, a jealous God. (Deuteronomy 4:24)

Don't let the word *jealous* trip you up, though. Today, jealousy is attributed to relationships in general, and we often think about a raging, irrational, jealous boyfriend or girlfriend flying off the handle upon finding his or her significant other cheating. But our current definition—however distorted by imperfect humans—does in fact accurately represent a characteristic of our King of Kings. The word *jealous* comes from the Latin word *zeal*. Merriam-Webster defines it as "one who is intolerant of rivalry or unfaithfulness and vigilant in guarding a possession."[7] Before you tie a negative, cultural view of the word *jealous* to your King, take a moment to comprehend this fact:

> *The creator of the universe, the God who hung the moon and the stars and can move mountains with just a word from His powerful voice, wants every single ounce of your attention and affection. This desire for your love and worship is so intense it is like a consuming, holy, pure fire.*

To worship our King with our intense relationships is to bring to the throne our passionate, romantic feelings that swell in our hearts and often-times overwhelm us to the point where we worship the guys in our lives instead of our Divine, Jealous God. This happens to the best of us when we are so in love and in the pre-intensity stage of the relationship, and all we want to do is spend every waking hour with our guy. What happens, then, is we begin to do what the Israelites did: worship an idol (our guy) rather than our amazing, loving, powerful King. By not allowing ourselves to drown in a sea of emotions that surround a newly-intensified relation-ship, we make room in our lives to delight in the Lord first, which is what brings us true fulfillment in relationships.

I like to look at healthy, intense relationships as a triangle. In the two blanks at the bottom corners of this triangle, write your name in one and the name of your guy in the other. If you aren't presently in relationship, that's okay. Just write "guy" in that blank. At the top of the triangle, write the word *God*.

It is imperative that we have our own, separate relationship with God and not rely on our boyfriend's, fiancé's, or husband's faith in order to worship Jesus. The names at the bottom of the triangle—your name and your guy's name—represent your individual faiths in the Divine, Jealous God. As you move up the triangle toward God, your faith grows stronger and your worship is more meaningful and individualized based on your personal needs and love for God. As your guy moves up the triangle toward God, the same happens for him. Though you might attend church together, pray together, and talk about your faith together, neither one of you should depend on the other's faith to sustain your own, individual worship of the Lord. A faith that depends on another human's relationship with the Lord is only as strong as the inevitable mistakes that human makes. It's a fact. Our relationship with the Lord is weakened when it is dependent on the faith of our significant other. Just as your faith is not always exceptionally strong, neither is his faith. We all fail God at some point. Therefore, you and I *must* develop our own stuff with God separate from our guy's stuff. We will discuss this a bit more in the journal section below.

What is really cool about the triangle illustration is what happens between us and our guy when we do, in fact, develop strong and individual relationships with Jesus. Put a finger on each point at the bottom of the triangle and run your fingers up the triangle toward the top point—toward God. What do you notice about how your fingers move? They actually move closer together, right? This illustration thrilled me to no end when I first heard it years ago. *You mean as I grow closer to my Divine, Jealous God, I then grown closer to my guy in a more meaningful way?* Yes! The relationship becomes . . .

> *centered on God and not on each other's faults or mistakes;*
> *more rich and meaningful as we let God speak to us individually and we*
> *then pour out purer love on one another;*
> *less codependent; and*
> *free to grow into what God made it to be.*

This is a lot of information to process. Take a few moments to journal through this concept below.

Journal 2
I WORSHIP AT THE THRONE OF MY KING

• Write out your thoughts regarding the concept of worshiping at the throne of your Divine, Jealous God. How does this concept sit with you based on our culture's definition of the word *jealous*?

_____

_____

_____

_____

• In the last chapter we discussed the Lord delighting in *us*. Thinking through Avery's outlook reminds me of my own need to take delight in the Lord. Read in your Bible Psalm 37:3–5. What are ways you personally can delight in the Lord? (For example: worshiping, sitting quietly in His presence, reading the Word)

_____

_____

_____

_____

_____

- Why do you think God gives us the desires of our hearts *after* we delight ourselves in Him?

- Write out your thoughts about the concept shown in the triangle illustration. Do you see the benefit of a relationship with your Divine, Jealous God separate from your guy's faith and relationship with Him?

Waiting at the Throne of the King (Sustained-Intensity Stage)

I'd like to skip over Shelby's Present-Intensity stage to discuss my own Sustained-Intensity stage case study and the concept of waiting at the throne of the King. I'd like to share my own experience as a married woman. We will pick back up with Shelby and her fiancé in the next section. I truly hope that you will file away the life lesson I learned four years into my marriage, and commit to place God rather than your boyfriend or fiancé on a pedestal.

I woke up and sat on the side of the bed after a peaceful night's sleep having no idea that Greg had tossed and turned next to me all night long. With a somber look on his face, Greg quietly whispered that he had something to confess to me. A lump immediately formed in my throat. Rather than walking away to avoid this uncomfortable moment, I allowed Greg to share his stricken heart, willing myself not to cry. He finished what he had to say and got up to take a shower, knowing that I needed a moment alone to process his words. The only thing I could actually process was an image of a tower crashing down with white, ivory-encrusted bricks shattering everywhere. Since the moment we met, Greg was perfect in my eyes, absolutely perfect. He grew up in a loving Christian home, attended a sweet little Christian school, and sustained an image in my mind of a purely perfect man who happened to love me, the one who made royal mistakes in her life.

As the weeks passed after the morning of Greg's confession, God showed me that this painful incident was a blessing. Though I never once questioned my marriage or Greg's incredible characteristics, this sudden realization of my husband's imperfection was one that forced me to question my own views of God, to take a look at the fact that I had placed Greg on the pedestal that was meant for my jealous God. This reminder to reflect was a very good thing.

ෆ I was forced to look at Jesus as the center of my world rather than viewing my guy as the definition of my existence.

ෆ I was thrown into a new reality that no human can live up to expectations of love, fulfillment, forgiveness, and adoration that should only be placed on our King.

ෆ I was placed right at the throne of my King, waiting for Him to redefine *who* is top priority in my life, because He is my Divine, Jealous God.

Whatever kind of intense relationship you are living out, take some time to evaluate whether you, like me, put your guy in a place in your life and heart that only God should inhabit. Just as I did in this transformational point of my faith, take a look at this passage from Colossians, and use this Scripture as a mirror to your own heart and affections.

> Since, then, you have been raised with Christ, set your hearts on things above, where Christ is seated at the right hand of God. Set your minds on things above, not on earthly things. For you died, and your life is now hidden with Christ in God. When Christ, who is your life, appears, then you also will appear with him in glory. (Colossians 3:1–4 NIV)

SET YOUR HEARTS ON THINGS ABOVE . . .

Have you yet to approach the throne of your Divine, Jealous God, waiting at His feet as you hand over your entire heart and allow Him to mold and shape you into a woman of pure passion and faith? This pure passion will pour into all of your relationships, especially your romantic ones, so that a selfless love develops and these relationships point out to the world around you—Jesus is King.

Have you developed a desire first for Jesus before you dive into sexual passion for your guy? Jesus will fill every ounce of your heart, thus allowing the special guy in your life to add to those spaces in your heart and not strive to fill any voids that he is incapable of filling. For most women, sex is more about the emotions of feeling needed and desired than it is a physical need. Setting our hearts on Jesus first protects our hearts and bodies from relationships based only on sex. Even the godliest of guys carry an intrinsic need for sex. When we set our hearts and wait at the throne of our King, we open our relationships to a new dynamic above and beyond one that is sexual, a rich relationship based on respect for each other's hearts and minds rather than just each other's bodies.

SET YOUR MIND ON THINGS ABOVE . . .

Do you commit your minute-by-minute thoughts to Jesus, checking in with Him throughout the day? That giddy feeling of a newly intensified romance can easily overtake our every thought throughout the day. It is fun to day-dream about our guy, thinking about where he is and what he is doing at that very moment even though we texted each other just a few minutes ago. These mushy-gushy feelings are fun and important for keeping the romance alive, but when they border on obsession and take our focus off of our ever Divine *and* Jealous God, we must find a balance throughout the day for where we set our minds. As I mentioned in the last chapter, a productive way to focus our thoughts in the heavenly direction is to pray for our guy. Wouldn't he be blessed to know you took to the throne his stressful day and conversed with Jesus on how you could encourage your guy? Staying in constant communication with our King helps us to be better girlfriends, fiancées, or wives to the men we love so much.

Take some time to journal through the passage of Colossians and con-sider how your own intense relationship could benefit from your setting your heart and mind on Jesus. Many of the concepts in this chapter go hand and hand with Love/Dating Part 1. I encourage you to flip back through the previous chapter to refresh your memory as we look at relationships that intensify.

Journal 3
I WAIT AT THE THRONE OF MY KING

Let's revisit Colossians 3:1–4, where Paul writes about heavenly things versus earthly things and how and what we set our affections and mind on. Very important: Even if you are not presently in a relationship, please do not skip these questions. Write the heavenly and earthly things that you see in past relationships or even how they would shape future relationships.

• With your romantic relationship in mind, make a list below of what could be considered heavenly things, or, as Paul writes, things that are "above" (Colossians 3:1.) (For example: Does your guy love Jesus? Does he give away his time or money to others? What is your relationship centered on?)

• Next, make a list of things that are regarded as earthly in your relationship. (For example: physical looks of your guy, how much money he makes, etc.

• How do your lists stack up against one another? Is one list longer than the other? I encourage you to evaluate how the items on the list of earthly things might possibly cause you to build up that ivory tower and place your guy rather than your Divine, Jealous God on a pedestal. Use the space below to journal through this concept of God on the pedestal rather than your guy.

Finding Focus on Him Alone (Present-Intensity Stage)

Our girlfriend Shelby and her fiancé did something very countercultural when their relationship intensified. While reality television encourages us to move in with our significant other (however loosely "significant other" might be defined), I admire Shelby and her fiancé for taking a hard stand to obey God's Word, which strictly states no sex before marriage (Hebrews 13:4; 1 Thessalonians 4:3, 4, 7; 1 Corinthians 7:2). This is a slippery slope especially if we have already experienced sex and our bodies are now attuned to those intimate feelings. It is especially easy to give into those feelings when we are deep in a committed, intense relationship that is headed toward marriage. We might think, *Oh, the wedding is right around the corner . . . we might as well . . .*

When Shelby gave her life over to Jesus and placed Him as her Divine, Jealous God, she stepped right back into that ideal, pure, white wedding gown that had been tarnished in previous relationships. When we bring our pasts to the throne, the Lord hands us our new virginity and offers us a new opportunity to stand pure before Him and our future spouses without even a hint of guilt. If you are weary of feeling that there is no going back on the times you slept around and there is no hope of feeling pure in that white wedding dress of the future, please know that Jesus makes all things new—even your virginity. When you decide to make Jesus your Lord and Savior, that white wedding dress is all yours, my friend. Step into the abundance of elegant white lace with confidence that you are a pure, beautiful bride for your future husband.

The following piece of Scripture was Shelby's motivation for establishing some ground rules in her intense relationship. She and her fiancé determined early on that it was to their benefit to obey God's commands.

I have loved you as the Father has loved Me. Abide in My love. Follow My example in obeying the Father's commandments and receiving His love. If you obey My commandments, you will stay in My love. I want you to know the delight I experience, to find ultimate satisfaction, which is why I am telling you all of this. (John 15:9–11 THE VOICE)

The Lord has a perfect plan regarding how we should live in a great intensified relationship. This is all dependent on our obeying His commands. It is all dependent on our staying right at the throne of our King and finding focus on how He wants us to carry out our relationships. Not everything is as crystal clear in the Bible as sex is. Things like whether or not it is acceptable to hold hands, kiss, or spend weekends together at his house are not exactly defined within Scripture. This is something that you and your man have to take to God through prayer and constant communication with Him. John 15:9–11 states that ultimate satisfaction in life starts with obedience to the Lord.

Whether or not you are in the present-intensity stage of a relationship, I encourage you to take some time to sort through which actions within a relationship are obedient to Him and which are not. If a certain part of your relationship (sex or anything else) hinders your constant focus at the throne of the King, it needs to be eliminated. Through prayer, take some time to set boundaries in your physical relationship with your man. These boundaries are different for each couple because each couple has different triggers that cause them to move into territory that is no longer obedient. For example, Shelby and her fiancé decided that they would not only refrain from sex but they wouldn't even sleep in the same bed when they went out of town on weekend vacations. Another interesting example is our friend Avery who did in fact meet and marry her husband, Emmet, after college. When their relationship intensified, Emmet decided that it was best that the couple stop things like kissing until their wedding day. Some would say this is extreme, but Avery and Emmet started to see the temptation to take things further when the kissing got hot and heavy. Neither of them wanted to tarnish the commitment they made to the Lord to keep their relationship on the straight and narrow. Plus, Avery knew that the Lord blesses those who obey His commands and follow His prompts as Jesus says in John 15.

As we discussed earlier in this chapter, the Lord as a jealous God not only wants our whole hearts as individuals, He also has the jealous desire for us to live in relationships that point to His goodness, His beauty, and His mercy. We can't do this when sex distracts us from growing closer on a spiritual and emotional level. Questions about the faith of our guy can distract us from having a relationship that is elevated to a level of pure focus on what pleases Jesus. While we don't want to criticize him, it's important to examine our guy's relationship with Jesus. It is a biblical fact that a husband should be the head of the family on a spiritual level (1 Corinthians 11:3) As women who desire to live out the Kingship of Christ in our intensified relationships, we've got to ask questions of our man in regard to His faith and relationship with God.

I thought it would be cool to ask my friends on Facebook what kinds of questions they would or did consider when examining their guy's faith. Take a look at some of their answers and consider asking yourself and your guy these questions.

Peggy: Is God first and foremost in his life? Was accepting Jesus as Lord and Savior a ticket to heaven or a life-changing event?

Savannah: Is he a man of integrity, and does his relationship with God continually grow?

Leanne: How would he explain Jesus to our future kids? Will he pray with me? Does he bring God up in everyday life or only in churchy settings?

Hannah: Who or what does he go to first for guidance? Does he have strong, godly mentors?

What do you think about the idea of examining not just your own faith but the faith of your guy in order to strengthen your intense relationship? I encourage you to find a couple in your community or church whom you respect; bounce these questions off of them, and pick their brains about their own marriage. Again, whether or not you are in a committed, intense relationship, it is so important to file away nuggets of truth regarding marriage for the future. This way you won't be playing catch up and learning hard lessons many years after the wedding.

Journal 4
I WILL FOCUS ON THE KING ALONE

- In light of our conversation regarding stepping into a new white wedding dress of purity regardless of your past mistakes and sin, read Isaiah 61:10 in your Bible. How does the passage speak to your heart?

- Take some time to reread the questions posed by my Facebook friends about examining your guy's faith. Rewrite some of the questions that stand out to you, and even come up with some of your own.

- What value do you see in focusing on these questions when taking a good look at your intense relationship?

Stress Diverted

Even though intense relationships are often exhilarating, they can also be stressful. As we try to get to know our guy on a deeper level, we can get tripped up by our own hang-ups and life baggage. In this chapter we focused much of our time on looking at the faith of our guy and the boundaries we set up within the relationship. Now let's take a little bit more time looking into a mirror at ourselves as I did in my personal girlfriend case study. Picking back up on Colossians 3, which we read earlier in this chapter, see if the rest of the passage strikes a chord with your heart and relates to how you personally worship, wait, and focus on your Divine, Jealous God. Please take a few minutes to read through Colossians 3:1–16 in your Bible. I especially love what verses 12–15 in *The Voice* Bible say:

> Since you are all set apart by God, made holy and dearly loved, clothe yourselves with a *holy way of life*: compassion, kindness, humility, gentleness, and patience. Put up with one another. Forgive. Pardon any offenses against one another, as the Lord has pardoned you, because you should act in kind. But above all these, put on love! Love is the perfect tie to bind these together. Let your hearts fall under the rule of the Anointed's peace (the peace you were called to as one body), and be thankful. (THE VOICE)

Just as we clothe ourselves in a pure, new, white wedding dress when our sins are forgiven by the blood of our Jesus, we are also commanded in the Word to clothe ourselves with *a holy way of life*. This holy way of living doesn't stop when we leave church on Sunday, and it especially doesn't stop when things intensify with our guy. These commands of the Bible are for our benefit and help us to remove stress from our relationships as we become women who . . .

readily forgive the mistakes of our guy;

love him as a reflection of how Jesus loves him; and

put our needs behind his needs of respect, affection, and honor.

By taking on this holy mind-set and living our lives as if we are set apart, both you and your guy will worship your Divine, Jealous God through this holy, intense relationship that points straight to His goodness, love and mercy.

Journal 5
I LAY IT ALL DOWN BEFORE THE THRONE

Below are some prayer point journal prompts. Finish these thoughts with your own words in a written prayer.

• *Father, my Divine, Jealous God, show me ways that I can honor and worship You alone . . .*

• *Lord, I thank You for this man You put in my life or for the man You may put in my life in the future . . .*

• *Father, here are some things I love about my intense relationship; take them and multiply the blessings . . .*

• *Lord, here are some concerns about my intense relationship; take them and transform this relationship to one that truly glorifies You . . .*

*Go to **www.liveitoutblog.com/stress-point** to watch
a video from Sarah on this chapter's Stress Point!*

CHAPTER 6

STRESS POINT:
FRIENDS AND FAMILY

SAVE THE DRAMA

Before I surveyed a group of my 20-something girlfriends, I was sure that I was the only one who dealt with friends and family stress. Apparently I was wrong. Our friends and family are people we love and hate at the same time. It is a weird paradox that I've yet to figure out, but as I've navigated through my twenties already, I'd like to share some of the lessons I've learned to hopefully save you a bit of stress. In the family arena, the tricky part is that they know all of our junk. They've lived our mistakes with us, they've seen us fall and get back up maybe a little bruised and broken. There is not much we can fake with our families, and I think that keeps me honest. In the friend arena, well, that is a different type of stress. In a decade of drama, our friends come and go. We may or may not keep in touch with our old high school crowd. Life transitions in your twenties most likely put you in a different place than your BFFs from seventh grade. This can cause awkward moments when you no longer have anything in common. The drama doesn't stop with our newer friends either. The pressure of taking classes or working a forty hour week makes it difficult to be available for our friends. The stress point of friends and family is a big topic, and we won't be able to cover it all in one chapter. But let's jump in together and see what we can stir up.

 ## Girlfriend Case Study #1

Hannah and Sarah (Me), two sisters whose parents set the expectation that they would be best friends despite wanting to tear each other's heads off as kids. I used to hate how my mom would say, "You *will* be your sister's best friend whether you like it or not!" With an eye roll and a sassy attitude, I would swallow whatever snide comment I was just about to throw at my little sister, Hannah. Now that we are adults, Hannah is my best friend, without a question. Though miles separate us, a phone call every evening on her way home from work puts me right by her side. We text each other with lyrics from our favorite songs and LOL knowing just what memory the other referred to with that song. The relationship is not without drama, though. Because of the deep comfort level between us, it's all too easy to slip up and smart off if I'm in a bad mood, since I know she won't desert me because of my sharp tongue. Other friends would walk away, but my sister never would.

 ## Girlfriend Case Study #2

Lindsay, a recent college grad reminiscing about a friendship turned upside down. Lindsay and Amy met each other freshman year and spent many hours doing what college friends do: they studied together, shopped, gossiped about boys, went to class, had mutual friends, you name it. As many college students also do, they spent late nights at the bar, then scarfed down "after hours" pizza on the floor of their shared dorm room. As the girls entered their senior year of college, Lindsay decided to put her faith in the Lord instead of filling once-empty spaces in her heart with drinking, partying, gossiping, and other activities that characterized her life during the previous three years of college. Amy didn't choose to travel down the path that Lindsay chose, and their relationship suffered. Living between these two worlds is a balancing act. One world values different things than the other. Today, Lindsay is determined to figure out how to hang out with her friends who don't yet know Jesus. She wants so badly to relate and show these friends how her life drastically changed when Jesus became her King.

 ### Girlfriend Case Study #3

Kelly, a twenty-eight-year-old who has spent the last several years cultivating some friendships and breaking away from others. Though she loves the diversity of having friends in various groups and life-stages, she finds herself spread thin and unable to give 100 percent to those she cares about. Plus, some of the drama that Kelly's friends bring to the table wears her out. As she evaluates the stress revolving around her relationships, Kelly realizes that the best kinds of friends are those who are low-maintenance in the drama department, and she sets out on a mission to be just that. Feeling free of the need to call or text her girlfriends at every turn, Kelly experiences a sense of reconnection with the Lord as she spends more time telling Him about her life drama and less time running to her girlfriends to vent.

Journal 1
IDENTIFY YOURSELF

- Do you see yourself in one of these girlfriend case studies? If not, journal out where you stand with friends and family these days.

_____

_____

_____

_____

- What do you love most about your family dynamic?

_____

_____

_____

_____

_____

- What do you love most about the different dynamics of your friendships?

_____

_____

_____

_____

_____

Worshiping at the Throne of the King

I would like for you to take a moment and write in the margins of this book your definition of a "normal" family. Go ahead, take a crack at it. It's kind of difficult, right? That is because there is no such thing as a normal family. I always jokingly say that if things were "normal" we wouldn't know what to do with ourselves. Every family is different, and whether or not we admit it aloud, our lives would be a bit off-kilter were it not for our family quirks. It is because of the quirks and idiosyncrasies of our loved ones that we learn to love others unconditionally just as God loves us.

How did you describe your family dynamic in Journal 1? Is your "normal" a family where your parents are divorced and you live with your mom? Is your "normal" a family that is defined by a community of friends who care for each other; spend holidays together; and share meals, laughs, and tears? For our purposes, family is defined by the people in your life that you care for, spend time with, and maybe even share drama with. Family might be the parents who raised you or it might be the friends who keep you honest and on the straight and narrow. When it comes to family, worshiping at the throne of the King means we celebrate these special people and don't waste the gift that they are to us we go about our everyday lives. Though flawed and only human, these people are used by God to give us a slight glimpse of one aspect of His character: He is the Eternal God. I equate God's eternalness to our topic of family and friend drama because it reminds us that though our relationship dynamics change and drama unfolds, our Eternal God is always with us. A neat synonym to *eternal* that is often used in the Bible is *everlasting*. Our Jesus is everlasting and eternal. Even through the stress point of dealing with our friends and family, we can always count on the fact that "Jesus Christ is the same yesterday and today and forever" (Hebrews 13:8 NIV). In a culture where trends constantly change, there is always some new gadget, and our friends come and go, we can rest assured that the Eternal God is our one constant.

Our friends and family who do, in fact, stick around through thick and thin are earthly examples of the love that Jesus—the Eternal God—shows us day in and day out. Those in our lives who know our dirt and can see into the deep, dark crevasses of our hearts yet still love us and refuse to leave us reflect the love of our God who will absolutely never walk away. The Eternal God is not affected by our slipups and flat-out sin. Though He might discipline us to help us learn our lesson, this is a promise in the Word that we must cling to:

> Be strong and of good courage, do not fear nor be afraid of them;
> for the LORD your God, He is the One who goes with you. He will
> not leave you nor forsake you. (Deuteronomy 31:6)

As we worship at the throne in light of the gift He gives us of people who love us unconditionally, one true way not to squander this gift is by respecting our family members. I live about a four-hour plane ride from my family, so that means that we only see each other a handful of times per year. The moment I book my plane ticket, my heart jumps with joy at the thought of seeing my mom and dad, eating my mom's homemade chili, and laughing my head off with my hilarious sister. The entire trip is built up in my head as one of those old Hallmark commercials; the ones where the perfect family sits around the fireplace sharing memories and smiling lovingly at each other. Granted, I know this is not realistic; I really do. But it sure does sound nice, doesn't it?

When I arrive at home and settle into the visit that I've fantasized so much about, everything is just great. And then comes that inevitable moment when someone makes a snide remark or brings up a past grudge, and the bottom falls out and things go south fast. In a matter of seconds my Hallmark moment goes right out the window.

After a few trips gone bad, I've come to realize that I need to own the fact that I am a willing participant in our family drama. Yes, I said it. I have a huge responsibility in the family drama, and it comes down to R.E.S.P.E.C.T. You see, now that I am an adult, I want to be treated as such. I have lived the days where I followed a curfew, was told how to wear my hair, and obeyed the rules laid out for me. I have also lived the days where I coexisted with a houseful of loved ones and perfected the art of taunting my little sister. Those days are long gone, yet it is so easy to slip back into old habits of disrespecting my family. I was reading a great verse in the Bible the other day that helped me put this newfound respect into perspective. In Matthew 22:37–40 Jesus says, "Love the Lord your God with all your heart and with all your soul and with all your mind. This is the first and greatest commandment. And the second is like it: 'Love your neighbor as yourself.' All the Law and the Prophets hang on these two commandments" (NIV).

It occurred to me while reading this that the term *neighbor* Jesus used also applies to our families. If we desire to sit before the throne and truly worship our Eternal God, we must love this very family that might drive us crazy. When we love our family out of obedience to Jesus, respect flows naturally out of that love. Now, this is not a magic formula for perfect family interactions, but it does guarantee to minimize the drama. The next time you fantasize about sitting around the fireplace drinking coffee and sharing pure, loving moments with your family, don't forget the respect. It's a hard pill to swallow, but the Lord will bless you for it; I promise.

Journal 2

I WILL WORSHIP AT THE THRONE

- Take a few minutes to journal through some ways you can take responsibility for family drama and show respect.

_____

_____

_____

- Read with me the beautiful flow of verses about our Eternal God from Psalm 93 in *The Voice*:

> The Eternal reigns, clothed in majesty; He is dressed *in power*; He has surrounded Himself with strength. He has established the world, and it will never be toppled. Your throne was established from the beginning of the world, O *God*, and You are everlasting. The waters have risen, O Eternal One; the sound of pounding waves *is deafening*. The waters have roared *with power*. More powerful than the thunder of mighty rivers, more powerful than the mighty waves in the ocean is the Eternal on high! *Your teachings are true*; Your decrees sure. Sacredness adorns Your house, O Eternal One, forevermore.

- Focus in on the words in this passage that describe God as eternal and everlasting, and journal through how this resonates with you.

_____

_____

_____

_____

- How does your family dynamic reflect, even in a small way, the love of your Eternal God?

_____

_____

_____

_____

_____

- Focus on verses 3 and 4. How is the drama in your life similar to the rising, turbulent waters and the deafening, pounding waves?

_____

_____

_____

_____

_____

- What does it mean to you that your Eternal God is mightier than the turbulence of the drama in your life?

_____

_____

_____

_____

_____

Waiting at the Throne of the King

So often we, as Christians, live in a little bubble, secluding ourselves from the world around us. We have our own Christian radio stations, bookstores, clubs, and coffeehouses. We make Christian friends and attend Christian schools. We listen to Christian bands and go to Christian concerts. But what is it that keeps us in our little bubble? Is it pride—do we think we are better than those *sinners*? Is it fear—are we concerned that our faith is not strong enough to withstand temptation? Is it intimidation—are we worried that we won't accurately talk about the gospel, so we don't even try? I know all three of these things keep me from stepping outside of my comfort zone and interacting with non-Christians. But lately, I've noticed this separation from the secular world may be keeping my friends from joining God in His work. These are people who could be inviting God into not only their own lives but the lives of their friends, families, and coworkers who don't yet know that our King is the center of life even during times of stress.

Once we choose to make Jesus our Lord and King, the Holy Spirit begins to transform our hearts. Our behaviors and spoken words that were once acceptable in our non-Christian crowds now stand in opposition to God's Word. We strive to live obediently—though slip-ups still occur. The challenge for us now is to build a firm foundation and to plant ourselves right at the throne of the King daily in order to pop the bubble of seclusion from non-Christians and share how Jesus drastically affects our lives, if we choose to let Him.

Lindsay inspires me in her desire to maintain her old friendships even though these long-time friends don't understand her new life choices. I see her sweet heart hurting for her friends because she knows her new life with Jesus is more fulfilling than the days of partying, gossip, and unhealthy living. Lindsay's faith gives her purpose. I also see Lindsay's bravery in her efforts to continue these friendships and not shy away in fear that her old friends will tempt her with things of her past. I like to say that Lindsay is *mixing it up.*

Definition of Mixing It Up: With a firm foundation of living out God's Word, praying to stay constantly connected with Him, and worshiping Him to place Jesus above all else, we take Jesus into the world that surrounds us and represent Him well.

ᘔ Mixing it up means we let our Eternal King bring out the best in us to affect change in the hearts of those in our lives who need to know about His love, forgiveness, mercy, and grace.

ᘔ By mixing it up we work alongside Jesus to bring out the best in others and live by example rather than pointing fingers and criticizing.

ᘔ Mixing it up means we are not offended by ungodly behaviors of those who don't know our King. Rather, we show others the love of Jesus by living our everyday lives in a way that please Him.

In the book of Acts, Jesus instructs His disciples to be His witnesses.

And you shall be My witnesses, first here in Jerusalem, then beyond
to Judea and Samaria, and finally to the farthest places on earth.
(Acts 1:8)

This critical bit of instruction to the men and women who followed Jesus during His three years of ministry came forty days after Easter Sunday, mere moments before Jesus ascended back into heaven to sit on His throne for eternity. God would soon empower those men and women with His Holy Spirit so they could go out without fear or trepidation, show love to others, and tell them about Christ. So what does this mean for you and me when it comes to how we interact with our friends, family, and those in our lives who aren't Christians?

It is difficult to grasp the role of the Holy Spirit because He is neither someone we can touch nor a figure we can picture in our minds. The Spirit is a gift that Jesus gives us automatically when we make the commitment to follow Him with our entire heart, mind, soul, and body. The Holy Spirit then gives us the strength to step outside of our Christian bubble, resist the temptations of the world, and mix it up with the very people who Jesus Himself created and loves dearly.

Waiting at the throne of the King means we allow the Holy Spirit to guide and direct us in our interactions with others in order to live out our faith and draw our friends to Jesus without pushing them away. This is only possible if we immerse ourselves in the Lord daily and allow Him to fill us with His love, peace, mercy, goodness, and joy. By filling our lives with the goodness of our Eternal King, we are able to pour out that love, peace, mercy, goodness, and joy upon our friends and family without the fear of succumbing to temptation; we are able to mix it up.

Here are some hypothetical situations that will encourage you to fill up first and then mix it up.

Fill Up: Your friends head out to the bar on a Thursday night and ask you to join them. Because you treasure their friendship, you decide to sit down with your Bible and let the Holy Spirit remind you to be filled with self-control.

> But also for this very reason, giving all diligence, add to your faith virtue, to virtue knowledge, to knowledge self-control, to self-control perseverance, to perseverance godliness, to godliness brotherly kindness, and to brotherly kindness love. For if these things are yours and abound, you will be neither barren nor unfruitful in the knowledge of our Lord Jesus Christ. For he who lacks these things is shortsighted, even to blindness, and has forgotten that he was cleansed from his old sins. (2 Peter 1:5–9)

Mix it up: You don't have any convictions against drinking, but you understand your limits and hate to say or do something you regret while drunk. So you join your friends with the commitment to limit the alcohol and focus less on the cocktails and more on the opportunity to hang out with your girlfriends.

Fill up: You serve on a committee for a fundraiser and you're having a blast getting to know the other women on the board. After a few meetings you notice one of the women runs her mouth constantly and is merciless in her gossip. Before the next meeting you take some time to journal through why you enjoy this group even though the gossip is getting on your nerves. You take some time to pray for guidance and ask your Eternal King to direct you on how to best handle this situation for His glory.

Mix it up: At the fundraiser meeting you end up right next to the gossip queen, who happens to say something about your best friend's breakup with her boyfriend. You take a deep breath and calmly explain that you don't appreciate her commentary. She might push back or even snub you, but the way you handle the conversation with grace sets a powerful example for the other women in the room listening to the conversation.

Fill up: It's the middle of the month and pay day isn't for a couple of weeks. You and your friends head to the mall to look around, though all of you are tight on cash. Everyone has their credit cards ready to charge away the shopping spree, but you remember the podcast you listened to online that taught about being frugal with your money in order to use it to bless others in need. In the back of your mind, you know your friends won't understand this concept.

Mix it up: While you truly have fun hanging out window-shopping, the other girls walk around with bags full of cute clothes. When the girls ask why you didn't just charge it, you take the opportunity to share how excited you are to save up in order to send money to the child you sponsor in Ecuador.

As we grow closer to our Eternal King and wait at His throne, our faith grows so that we are comfortable not isolating ourselves from our nonbelieving friends. Day by day as we fill up at His throne, we develop a firm foundation of who God is and how His Word teaches us to live our lives and not waiver, no matter who we hang out with.

Journal 3

I WILL WAIT AT THE THRONE

• Look up these verses in your Bible and write out how each one describes our King.

Hebrews 13:8

_____

_____

_____

Hebrews 7:3

_____

_____

_____

Psalm 102:27

_____

_____

_____

Psalm 72:17

_____

_____

_____

- Regarding your relationships with friends who don't share your love for Jesus, how do these descriptions of the Eternal King aid you or encourage you to stand firm in your faith?

_____

_____

_____

_____

_____

_____

- What are some ways you can mix it up with your friends and family after you have filled up?

_____

_____

_____

_____

_____

_____

Finding Focus on Him Alone

So far in this chapter we've covered ways to minimize family and friend drama as we worship and wait at the throne of our Eternal King. One more drama minimizer I'd like to throw out to you is the concept of being a low-maintenance friend; a friend who seeks to love and cherish her girlfriends without adding any unnecessary pressure or expectations to the relationship. This type of friend is ready and willing to get in the trenches of life with us; she is full of encouragement and advice, yet she also gives us space if that's what we need. If you desire to be this type of friend because you long for low-maintenance friends yourself, I propose you first place your focus on your Eternal King.

Take a moment to revisit the verse in Matthew that we covered at the beginning of this chapter, honing in especially on the first half of the passage.

> Love the Lord your God with all your heart and with all your soul and with all your mind. This is the first and greatest commandment. And the second is like it: "Love your neighbor as yourself." All the Law and the Prophets hang on these two commandments. (Matthew 22:37–40 NIV)

Love your God with all your heart, soul, and mind. Let Jesus, the Eternal King, pour His never-ending acceptance into your *heart* so you are free from striving for the acceptance of your friends. Let Jesus, your Eternal King, cover your *soul* with a blanket of infinite security so your needs are met by Him rather than by your friends. Let Jesus, your Eternal King, occupy your *mind* with thoughts of hope and joy so that if and when your friends let you down you know that your God will never leave or forsake you. A laser-sharp focus on who is most important—the Eternal King—sets us up naturally as low-maintenance friends.

If you have yet to get to the point in your relationship with Jesus where you look to Him as your Eternal King first and as a friend second, I encourage you to ask the Lord to reveal Himself to you in this light. By simply asking God to show us that Jesus is our friend, we open our heart to see Him as the One we run to with our hurt hearts, our exciting news, our tears, our frustrations, our fears, and our joy. The Lord longs for us to live in a state of intimacy with Him where we trust Jesus enough to share with Him even the minute details of our day. Living in this heart-to-heart friendship with the Lord gives us perspective on our earthly friendships.

I love how the book of John gives us glimpses into the relationships between Jesus and those He did life with. Can you even imagine what it would be like to hang out in person with the King of Kings? Though we have the perspective of the entire New Testament to give us the full picture of just who Jesus is, would we have fully grasped that the very man we just ate dinner and shared a story about our stressful day with was God in the flesh? I'm not sure I can answer that question, but I'm blessed by the stories that John shares. I pray that you will absorb these Scriptures and take a few moments to let your mind wander back two thousand years and dream what it would have been like to . . .

Lean against Jesus after a large meal and just chill.

The disciple John felt so comfortable with his friend Jesus that he reclined back in his dinner seat and simply relaxed with his Lord (John 13:23). *Is your relationship with your Eternal King and Friend so intimate that you sit quietly with Him after a long day and enjoy His presence?*

See Jesus weep and be heartbroken.

Mary and Martha ran to their friend, Jesus, after their brother Lazarus died. Mary and Martha's Friend and Eternal King wept not because He was incapable of healing Lazarus but likely because He was overwhelmed by the grief and pain of Mary and Martha (John 11:1–27). *Does it surprise you that Jesus cares about your hurt heart?*

Dance with Jesus at a party.

Jesus didn't shy away from fun. Instead He enjoyed celebrations like weddings and even cared enough to turn water into wine so the guests wouldn't turn on the host of the party (John 2:1–12). *Do you see Jesus as a real person who loves to let loose and enjoy Himself?*

When He is the One we turn to for encouragement and guidance, it takes the pressure off of our friends to fulfill that deep need. When we live out the idea that Jesus weeps, dances, hangs out with us, and truly enjoys our company, we are less likely to entertain hurt feelings when our friends let us down. Earthly friendships are absolutely necessary and biblical, because God made us as relational beings. By clinging tight to our Eternal King and Friend, allowing Him to satisfy us, we can be the type of friend that we desire to be—low-maintenance.

I threw out a question on Facebook about being a low-maintenance friend and this is what my girlfriends had to say:

Alexandra: A low-maintenance friendship is one where I rarely see my friend due to hectic schedules, yet we remain thick as thieves via text or phone. We are able to pick right up where we left off and no one takes offense by the fact that the other is busy.

Heidi: My low-maintenance friendships are rooted in love. This love is very forgiving of each other's busy-ness and the long distance between us. We are content with each other and overjoyed when we are able to carve out time to spend with each other.

Sunni: My most cherished low-maintenance friend is one that when we are bored and want to hang out, she comes over—sweatpants and sans makeup—to my dirty house and meets me wherever I am in my life drama.

Elle: A low-maintenance friend is one who shares *and* listens and doesn't require constant care.

"The most beautiful discovery true friends make is that they can grow separately without growing apart."

—Elizabeth Foley

I've learned throughout the years that if I want good friends who understand my crazy life, I have to be a friend who respects their need for space. I also need to be willing to pick up where we left off when my friend's need for space dissipates. I wasn't always this type of friend, and I know that I've severed some relationships because I expected too much from my girlfriends. But as I grow closer to my Eternal King and Friend, He teaches me grace and mercy that I then impart to my friends. Take a few moments to journal through the topic of friendship and work through how you can be a friend who loves Jesus first.

Journal 4

I FIND MY FOCUS ON HIM ALONE

• What is your personal definition of low-maintenance friendship?

_____

_____

_____

_____

_____

_____

_____

_____

• How do you think looking to Jesus as your Eternal King and Friend will enrich your earthly friendships?

_____

_____

_____

_____

_____

_____

_____

_____

_____

- Pick one of the examples from the book of John that we discussed in this section and look up the passage in your own Bible. Put yourself in that passage and imagine what it would have felt like to be Jesus' friend at that time.

- Make a few notes about your emotions as you journal through the idea of Jesus as your Eternal King and Friend.

Stress Diverted

Living out the Kingship of Christ in the area of family and friend relation-ships isn't something that happens overnight. We won't wake up tomor-row to a life where every friendship is beautiful and every family member treats us kindly just because we made the decision to give this stress point over to our King. Our friends and family might not understand our journey toward placing Jesus, our Eternal King, at the center of our lives. I've even seen relationships break down because one friend is jealous that the other places Jesus on His throne. These types of friends or family expect us to place them as our priority, and that stands directly against what the Bible teaches us.

> He who loves father or mother more than Me is not worthy of Me. And he who loves son or daughter more than Me is not worthy of Me. And he who does not take his cross and follow after Me is not worthy of Me. (Matthew 10:37–38)

This passage isn't an easy one to swallow, but it points to the hard truth about placing Jesus as our priority. By taking up our cross we are putting aside everything that used to be of utmost importance in our life, including our friends and family, and following our Eternal King. It hurts to think that best friends or siblings or parents can't be at the top of our list, but there is great benefit and blessing if we love Jesus more than our earthly friends and family. When we let Jesus have our full attention and our whole heart, He teaches us how to love our friends and family in a way that is outside of our own capabilities.

When our sister or brother annoys us to no end . . . Jesus gives us the patience to refrain slamming the door in frustration.

When our parents don't understand our life choices and refuse to support our dreams . . . Jesus gives us the strength to continue to respect them while prayerfully pursuing that life choice.

When our girlfriend forgets our birthday . . . Jesus teaches us to forgive and move on.

When an acquaintance gossips about our latest life drama . . . Jesus reminds us not to return the favor with more backstabbing.

Take time today to evaluate your relationships and ask your Eternal King to show you ways you can love your friends and family so deeply that they see Jesus in you and want more of Him. Worship at the throne by celebrating the people in your life that God has blessed you with. Wait at the throne and soak in Him in order to fill up. Then, go ahead and mix it up with your friends who need to know that Jesus loves them. And finally, point your sole focus on your Eternal King and Friend who gives you satisfaction and fulfillment so you don't need to completely rely on your friends and family to meet your needs.

Journal 5

I LAY IT ALL DOWN BEFORE THE THRONE

Below are some prayer point journal prompts. Finish these thoughts with your own words in a written prayer.

- *Father God, my Eternal King, I confess that there are ways that I can be a better friend, daughter or sister. I want to please You by loving my friends and family well . . .*

_____

_____

- *Lord, I thank you for my friends and family who You generously place in my life . . .*

_____

_____

- *Father, continue to show me how I need to place You as my priority above my friends and family . . .*

_____

_____

*Go to **www.liveitoutblog.com/stress-point** to watch a video from Sarah on this chapter's Stress Point!*

CHAPTER 7

STRESS POINT:
MONEY
RETAIL THERAPY
DOESN'T CUT IT

Let's face it: the topic of money is painful. If you're like me, you might even feel like *money* is a dirty word. Credit card debt and poor spending habits are common to many young women. You're certainly not alone if you taste the bitterness of the word *debt* on your tongue. But when we realize that God alone blesses us with money, it's easier to alleviate this stress point.

 Girlfriend Case Study #1

Rebecca Bloomwood from the movie *Confessions of a Shopaholic*. Rebecca is a young professional with a serious shopping addiction who pads her résumé and, ironically, lands a job as a journalist with a financial magazine. She is hopeful this job will force her to break her addiction and pay down her enormous credit card debt. Rebecca is beautiful and always fashionably dressed, and I have a sneaking suspicion that we all want to be like her, or at least to experience her walk-in closet. But it's key to remember that she acquired that fantastic wardrobe via high-dollar spending sprees and extremely high-interest credit card charges. Maybe you can see yourself in this quote from the movie: "You know that thing when you see someone cute and he smiles and your heart kind of goes like warm butter sliding down hot toast? Well that's what it's like when I see a store. Only it's better."

We all know what's at the bottom of this felt need for expensive shoes or must-have handbags; Rebecca thrived on the image she portrayed through the high-end shopping bags she slung over her shoulder as she went from store to store. She struggled to show others her value and net worth based on the image that she was somebody—at least based on the labels on her burdensome handbag. But once Rebecca found herself broke, that image was only as good as the credit card the sales clerk had to slice up in front of a store full of people. This line in the movie says it all: "They said I was a valued customer. Now they send me hate mail."

Rebecca treasured her role as a "valued" customer. She wasn't a shopaholic; she was addicted to the thrill of the image her expensive taste portrayed. In the end, her mind-set with regard to money only tarnished her American Express Gold Card image.

 ### Girlfriend Case Study #2

Sarah (Me), the girl who never denies herself "retail therapy." There was a time in my life when I was very much alone. Without a job to keep me busy but with a perfectly good credit card, I filled this void of loneliness with weekly, ahem, make that *daily* trips to Target. Seems innocent enough, right? That's exactly what I told myself every time I darkened the doorways of this all-too-tempting store. The void I was so desperately trying to fill felt less piercing when I was armed with a new tube of shiny pink lip gloss. But my low-cost fix didn't end with glossy lips. The latest line of junk jewelry was sure to brighten my dark day. Though I was not spending money in super chic boutiques on Madison Avenue, the daily trips to Target in small-town-USA added up—and the bottom line wasn't pretty. The cheap, fun clothing didn't seem as gratifying when the credit card bill hit me squarely between the eyes. Emotional spending is the way I found myself financially in the red.

 ## Girlfriend Case Study #3

Samantha: an executive accountant and the youngest female on her company's board. High pressure and long hours leave little time or energy for high-end trips to Gucci or cheap thrills from Target. Samantha spends her free time on the subway, pining away for the amazing vacay she's got coming up—next year. No, not this year, since she's entirely too busy and in the process of saving up. Other than work, Samantha's priority is making money and squirreling it away for that that future, one-time, all-out splurge. Samantha finds it fun to dream and plan and obsess over that moment of gratification when all her hard work will culminate in one glorious ski vacation in Switzerland—or, alternatively, a beach trip to Fiji. When the fun's all over, the glare of misplaced priorities will beat down painfully. Once the money is blown, albeit in a fun and exciting way, it'll be time for Samantha to start dreaming of the next thrill down the road. Samantha never gives one thought to saving for her future financial security or donating money to help the charity for which she attended that fabulous ball. A never-ending cycle of dreams, followed by highs and then lows, keeps Samantha in a place of frustration and discontent. She doesn't bother to evaluate her priorities and can't seem to explain her thoughts on spending.

Journal 1

IDENTIFY YOURSELF

• With which girlfriend do you most identify? Why?

• What money stress are you dealing with at this moment?

• What exactly is it that's stressing you out?

Worshiping at the Throne of the King

My personal case study isn't unique. Do you, like me, find yourself constantly reaching out for something to fill an emotional void in your life? Long before the sheen from that eight-dollar tube of lip gloss rubs off, the void that I think has been filled is drained again. That very word *void* leaves a pit in my stomach as I type it out. By the same token, it delights me to type the simple word *fill*.

Jesus can and will fill our voids with lavish amounts of His power, strength, and love. Take some time to evaluate the voids in your life, and think back to those times when you rushed off to find some cheap, instant gratification, to a place where cute earrings and a color-of-the-season handbag thrilled your socks off—for the moment. What drove you to that moment? What life event or circumstance drove you to crave instant gratification in the first place? Here are some possibilities:

Void: Loneliness. Your boyfriend recently sat you down and had the "let's be friends" talk.

Void: Doubt. "Everyone" else at the office picks up huge bonuses as they reach sales goals. You don't quite reach your quota. Are you really cut out for this job?

Void: Dissatisfaction. That dream you had as a little girl of living "the life"—complete with a high-powered job, luxury home, and fast-paced social life—isn't your reality.

Void: Self-consciousness. You were never told you were the pretty one in the family. Nope, that fell to your older sister.

Oh, how quickly that shopping cart can overflow with cheap thrills and temporary void-fillers. I can see it now: the trendy sweater that promises to fill the void of jealousy, the darling ballet flats that intend to fill the void caused by grief or loss, the must-have T-shirt that makes an unsuccessful stab at filling the void caused by heartache from a lack of emotional support from Mom. Who couldn't have a field day at Target? But the

151

adrenaline high would begin to fade before we even tried on the clothes and ripped off the sales tags.

Continuous cycles of wants and needs repeat indefinitely. There's always going to be someone prettier than you, someone smarter, skinnier, more talented, or higher paid. There's always going to be that next coveted pair of jeans, next season's must-have fashion items, the latest version of the ever-evolving cell phone. To break the cycle, we need to remember that Jesus alone can truly satisfy our needs. Hand over your voids to Him, and that ache in your heart will vanish as you worship Jesus, your El Shaddai. *El Shaddai* translates into an amazing phrase: "God is the all-sufficient One" or "Almighty God." In the book of Genesis, God revealed himself to Abram as El Shaddai. Abraham and Sarah desperately wanted a child. At the old age of ninety-nine, Abraham, whose name at that time was Abram, heard God say to him:

> "I am Almighty God [El Shaddai]; walk before Me and be blameless.
> And I will make My covenant between Me and you, and will multiply
> you exceedingly." (Genesis 17:1–2)

I personally like to take this word *Shaddai* one step further: Jesus, my El Shaddai, is over the top; He's more than sufficient, more than enough for me. And He's more than enough for you, too, my friend. As we see later in Genesis, God showed Himself as more than enough when He made Abraham the father of the nation of Israel. Abraham didn't just have *one* child; God blessed him with many, many children, and Israel grew to be a great nation.

Look at your life as a cup, and ask yourself, *With what or whom will I fill this cup?* For me, as I've indicated, it's too often been that cheap tube of glittery lip gloss displayed so enticingly at the drugstore. Sure, I feel chic and renewed when I slather that shimmer on my lips after a tough day at the office. But since it is cheap after all, that shimmer wipes away with my first sip of Diet Dr. Pepper. Sometimes I attempt to fill my cup with acceptance by others. Do you try to fill your cup—your voids—with the love, adoration, and attention of other people in your life? They probably don't keep you content either. Before you know it, the liquid has evaporated once again. When we turn to people to fill our cup, the endless cycle of drain and refill becomes a burden on the person on whom we're struggling to depend.

Our El Shaddai has His own cup, one that's infinitely deep and never in need of replenishment. His cup alone will fulfill our need for satisfaction, love, companionship, and positive self-image. There's never an end to what He will pour into our lives when we accept Him as our Savior and Lord. Let's come to Him now with an open heart, ready to receive and be satiated with the fullness and meaning He waits to pour into us. When we allow God to fill our voids, anything our human loved ones add is icing on the cake.

El Shaddai, our God who is infinitely more than enough, is ready for you to come to Him with that empty cup. All He asks is that you be vulnerable enough with Him to reveal your voids.

Cup: Loneliness. Jesus will never leave you or forsake you; that's a promise straight from the Bible (Deuteronomy 31:6; Hebrews 13:5).

Cup: Doubt. Jesus has a plan for you that goes well beyond what you could ever imagine (Jeremiah 29:11–14).

Cup: Dissatisfaction. Worldly things gratify only for the moment. But in Christ may be found a boundless supply of the fruit of His Spirit—like love, joy, peace, and patience—that can satisfy your every craving (Galatians 5:22–23; John 10:10).

Cup: Fear of being unloved. A paraphrase of the well-loved verse John 3:16 might read like this: For God so loved you, (add your name), that He sent His One and only Son. God loves you with a love that can only be described as beyond abundant. It's boundless (Romans 8:31)!

Cup: Self-consciousness. You're beautiful to Jesus, sufficient for and delightful to Him just as He made you. The King is enthralled with your beauty and delighted in your presence (Psalm 45:11; Zephaniah 3:17).

Right here, right now, pick up your empty cup and come before Jesus. Tell Him exactly what these voids mean to you, being frank and vulnerable. Then be open for God to pour Himself abundantly into your life.

Journal 2
I WILL WORSHIP AT THE THRONE

The following passage teaches us about the fullness of God, which we take part in when we trust Christ with our life.

> That Christ may dwell in your hearts through faith; that you, being rooted and grounded in love, may be able to comprehend with all the saints what is the width and length and depth and height—to know the love of Christ which passes knowledge; that you may be filled with all the fullness of God. (Ephesians 3:17–19)

• If He stands ready to fill us with love that is wide, deep, and high, don't you think He'll handle our money stress points? Thoughts?

• The Lord has His own super-sized measuring cup. From it we can allow Him to satisfy the emotional needs we've tried to quench with money. Is it difficult to open yourself up to this concept? Why do you suppose that is?

- Take a look at verse 19 and check out the verb tense used in the word *fill*. A way to look at this word is "that which has been filled." Did you catch that? When we choose to trust in Christ as our Savior, we've already been filled with God's abundant fullness. The voids that we attempt to fill on our own are, in reality, superficial. List the voids in your life that you need to fill with God's readily available fullness.

- Why do you think it's so hard to hand these voids over to Him?

Waiting at the Throne of the King

Taking, or *making*, time to be with the Lord can be a difficult thing, especially if you're a busy woman, working to stay afloat. It may be difficult, yes, but it's so worthwhile! Setting aside this time and keeping the appointment allows Him to speak to our hearts about how we're spending our money and why we're making these purchases. Like Rebecca, we all at some point buy material things to show the world our worth. It may be that sporty Mercedes that plunged you so much deeper into the hole. Or the high-end Ferragamo purse or the Tiffany bracelet, purchased solely to keep up with the girls. What about your townhouse in the posh part of town (for which you had to take out a huge mortgage in order to look like you were living "the life")? These extreme examples highlight our need to wait on the Lord as He shows us where our heart is—and where it should be.

Oftentimes we want others to recognize our personal value or the value of our contributions, forgetting that we're already of infinite worth to God—the only One who really counts. That's right: *You* are of great importance to God, no matter what you buy, where you work, or where you vacation. That's all that matters. End of story. I would hate to find myself in heaven one day, hearing Jesus say to me, "You did an alright job with the time I gave you in life. But why did you put so much effort into what others thought of you? Didn't you know that you're the apple of *My* eye and that this is all that matters?"

Godly success starts with knowing His Word and letting it speak to your heart. When you're tempted to show off your latest high-ticket fashion item to prove your worth to your girlfriends, rest and wait. Remain secure in the knowledge that no shopping spree can ever boost your value to match your worth to Jesus. Two verses from the book of Matthew speak directly to this concept:

Therefore I say to you, do not worry about your life, what you will eat or what you will drink; nor about your body, what you will put on. Is not life more than food and the body more than clothing? Look at the birds of the air, for they neither sow nor reap nor gather into barns; yet your heavenly Father feeds them. Are you not of more value than they? Which of you by worrying can add one cubit to his stature? (Matthew 6:25–27)

For the purpose of this discussion, the word *worry* means to fret over how we'll pay for our expensive vacation with our girlfriends or which decorative mirror will most effectively spice up our living room. As this verse points out, if the Lord expends His concern on birds, how much more care will he invest in us! Jesus would tell us that there's nothing intrinsically wrong with having nice things. I like nice things, and my guess is that you do too. But when we worry excessively about how far these items will advance our social standing, we've gone overboard. The King of Kings, the Creator of the universe, your El Shaddai already holds you in high standing. No need to run around collecting things to address an already-met need.

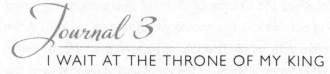

I WAIT AT THE THRONE OF MY KING

You don't need a telescope, a microscope, or a horoscope to realize the fullness of Christ, and the emptiness of the universe without him. When you come to Him, that fullness comes together for you, too. His power extends over everything. (Colossians 2:10 MSG)

• Is it intimidating for you to picture yourself approaching the throne of the King, "presumptuously" expecting to access His fullness? In your mind, what does that fullness mean?

• As the King of Kings and Creator of all, Jesus' all-encompassing power is the reality of our world—and, should we choose to tap in to it, the reality of our life. Why wouldn't we want to hand over the manner in which we spend money, along with the emotional voids that drive our behavior, to our El Shaddai? Do you prefer to maintain control in this area? Work this out on paper with your King, and take a moment to journal your thoughts below.

_____

_____

_____

_____

• We've talked about voids and cups. Take some time to list some of the voids in your life. Be real. Be honest. In what ways do you need your El Shaddai to fill your cup?

_____

_____

_____

_____

_____

_____

_____

Finding Focus in Him Alone

I'm wondering if you can relate to Samantha's situation, just as I did. Who doesn't love a dream vacation? As I've mentioned before, through in-depth reading of the Scripture, I'm convinced that the Lord doesn't forbid us to acquire nice things. On the contrary, He Himself often takes the initiative in blessing us with the finer things in life. Key phrase: *it's God alone who blesses us with the objects of our dreams.* All things come from Him. But I'll also go out on a limb to say that He tends to bless those who obey Him and make Him their top priority. We might even say that the blessings might not be material things. When our priority is pleasing God, He often pours into our life things like joy, peace, and contentment. It's in the order of priorities that our friend Samantha finds herself lost. She has pined away for high-dollar thrills to the point of obsession. Only after she realizes that her dreams are failing her can Samantha recognize that His blessings are infinitely more valuable than any material thing she has obsessed over.

Life gets less complicated when every penny we save and every financial move we make is weighed against its capacity to bring us closer to the Lord. The first step is to simply give away our hard-earned money. *Whoa, Whoa, Whoa!* you must be saying. How did we get *there* so fast? Yes, this is a radical approach for some of us. But if we claim Jesus as our Lord and El Shaddai, we must also adhere to the words of the Bible, commanding us to give ourselves 100 percent to Him.

The following verse about a poor widow should convince each of us to give our all (not every scrap of our stuff but our whole heart and allegiance)—not just when it's convenient for us but all the time:

Now Jesus sat opposite the treasury and saw how the people put money into the treasury. And many who were rich put in much. Then one poor widow came and threw in two mites, which make a quadrans. So He called His disciples to Himself and said to them, "Assuredly, I say to you that this poor widow has put in more than all those who have given to the treasury; for they all put in out of their abundance, but she out of her poverty put in all that she had, her whole livelihood." (Mark 12:41–44)

The widow gave to God out of sheer love and obedience. What's keeping us from giving out of the same kind of heart? I don't want this to turn into a sermon about tithing, but this step needs to be a part of the natural progression of our Christian growth and maturity. When our eyes are trained on the King, money isn't a priority; giving back to Him is.

When every ounce of our being is wrapped up in obsessing over money, the concept of giving a significant portion to the Lord strikes us as crazy. But when we approach tithing with a pure heart, we don't begrudge the dent in our monthly income. Once this becomes habitual for you, your friends will be mystified—even many of your Christian friends. This is an utterly foreign concept to many. But take a look at this verse in 2 Corinthians, and take heart:

But this I say: He who sows sparingly will also reap sparingly, and he who sows bountifully will also reap bountifully. So let each one give as he purposes in his heart, not grudgingly or of necessity; for God loves a cheerful giver. And God is able to make all grace abound toward you, that you, always having all sufficiency in all things, may have an abundance for every good work. (2 Corinthians 9:6–8)

What does all this sowing and reaping have to do with me? you may ask. It may surprise you to discover that there is a direct connection. Whenever we give generously, we'll be rewarded generously. That reward might come immediately, or it may arrive in the future. The reward may be tangible, but most likely it will be intangible. I want God to see me as a cheerful giver, don't you?

This passage encourages us to stop holing our money away for that fashion-forward handbag that will be worth the investment for all of five minutes. Our cheerful heart will obey God's direction regarding where, when, and how much to give. This takes a single-minded focus on His voice, a focus we can only attain when we're willing to invest ourselves in worshiping, waiting, and focusing on the King.

Journal 4
I FIND MY FOCUS IN HIM ALONE

No one can serve two masters, for either he will hate the one and love the other, or he will be devoted to the one and despise the other. You cannot serve God and money. (Matthew 6:24 ESV)

• The Greek word for "serve" in this passage is *douleuo*, which means "to be a slave to"—a slave to money, in this context. Ouch! In what ways are you presently a slave to money?

• Let's try an experiment that will help you pinpoint where your focus is on a day-to-day basis. Make a list of your top five "guilty pleasure" purchases—items unnecessary to everyday living. Record the approximate number of times you purchase each item during the course of four months. Then write down the approximate dollar amount of each item. My list is below:

_____ Cheap, pink, shiny lip gloss: 3 times, $8.00 each

_____ Coffee from a coffee shop: 10 times, $5.00 each

_____ Books, books, and more books: 4 times, $15.00 each

_____ Quarts of Ben & Jerry's ice cream: 8 times, $6.00 each

_____ Cute, funky, cheap shoes or jewelry: 10 times, $19.00 a pop

_____ Grand Guilty Pleasure Total: $372. Over the course of a whole year that extrapolates to $1,116. Yikes!

Now it's your turn. Go ahead and make your list. See what you come up with! This list will give you an idea of how much of your money goes to the kinds of things you typically focus on to fill your voids. How much money could you save if instead you ran to the Lord to fill your cup and ease your desire for "guilty pleasures"?

• By getting an idea of how we spend our money in attempt to fill our cup, we can get a grip on the allure of money. We can then better understand the temptation to become enslaved by money, spending and splurging rather than worshiping and focusing on our King. Has this exercise helped you to take a hard look at what you spend your money on? Why or why not?

- How can giving away your money in tithing 10 percent to your church, giving to other ministries, or simply handing a homeless person some cash free you of this bondage to money?

_____

_____

_____

_____

- As we discussed in 2 Corinthians 9:6–8, the Lord loves a cheerful giver. Is it hard for you to put the two words _cheerful_ and _giving_ together in the same sentence? If so, why? If not, journal through ways the Lord has blessed you in the past when you've freely given away your money.

_____

_____

_____

_____

_____

_____

_____

_____

Stress Diverted

Hopefully we've covered a few of the aspects of money management that have previously stressed us out. When we look at money as something other than a means to fill a void or express our value, we come to a point where we're glad to give a portion to the Lord for Him to use as He sees fit. There's no magic formula here. Managing money is a daily stress point over which each of us will continue to do constant, head-on battle (though hopefully we'll find the intensity reduced from full-on frontal attacks to skirmishes). So let's rely on Scripture as our weapon of choice as we engage in battle against the temptation to worship money and the quickly depreciating allure of that oh-so-cool sports car.

Once we've made the decision to take our money stress to the throne of the King, it's easy to let anxiety creep back in. Stress over credit card bills can throw us into a tailspin of self-medicating through retail therapy. But waiting at the throne of the King is a continual process; it's not a one-time-only deal so much as it is a day-by-day and even minute-by-minute process. He cares about the minute and boring details that stress you out, with the caveat that they're neither minute nor boring to him. The King of Kings who walked on water can handle your stress by helping you pay off the debt you've recklessly accrued. When these anxieties find their way into your daily routine, wait at the throne of the King and present it all to Him in prayer. Take a look at the journal section at the end of the chapter for prompts for praying about money. Let them be a springboard to prayers of your own, and then pray authentically, with total vulnerability, before God. He wants to hear what you have to say and to help you deal with your needs in ways you can't even begin to imagine.

Journal 5
I LAY IT ALL DOWN BEFORE THE THRONE

Below are some prayer point journal prompts. Finish these thoughts with your own words in a written prayer.

• *Lord, I acknowledge that You're my El Shaddai, even though it can be hard for me to trust that You're truly enough in these areas of my life . . .*

\
\

• *Lord, I'm stressed about money and bills. I commit this stress to You, knowing that You'll both guide and comfort me . . .*

\
\

• *Lord, I don't want to be a slave to money and expensive, guilty pleasures. I want to serve You alone—nothing and no one else. Free me from the bondage of compulsive spending . . .*

\
\

• *Lord, I know You don't want me to stress about anything. I know You take care of all my needs. Cover me with this assurance . . .*

\
\

*Go to **www.liveitoutblog.com/stress-point** to watch
a video from Sarah on this chapter's Stress Point!*

CHAPTER 8

STRESS POINT:

STEPPING OUT ON YOUR OWN

MISS INDEPENDENT

Stepping out, taking the risk to dive into this crazy world as an adult, as Miss Independent (cue Kelly Clarkson), can be totally scary. We like to think we are self-sufficient and not at all apprehensive about living out on our own, out from under the wings of the grown-ups in our lives. I remember when I moved into my first apartment post-college. It was a seven-hundred-square-foot space that was mine to decorate, leave messy, and clean up only *if* I felt like it. Exciting . . . until it came time to pay rent for the first time. Yikes. After writing the check I hurried off to work. Suddenly the fact that I must work my tail off in order to live became all too real. That invincible feeling of independence soon faded when tough, grown-up decisions filled my plate. The things I once left up to my parents, I was now required to figure out on my own. Miss Independent turned into little Miss

Indecisive, Miss Afraid—someone who was not the least bit confident that she could make it as a "big girl."

To explore this stress point, we will look at the feelings of apprehension about moving out on our own and how to fully live out our new role as Miss Independent. A true woman who clings to her King, Jesus, knows that she is never truly independent, but completely dependent on the Lord for guidance, direction, protection, and emotional support. You might not yet live out on your own. You might still depend on the support of other adults in your life: parents or family members who take you under their wing, and that's okay. In a world where jobs are hard to come by and money is tight, some of us might even still live at home. I hope you will take the words of this chapter as encouragement to take that risk and move out on your own—fully dependent on Jesus—when the time is right.

 ## Girlfriend Case Study #1

Melanie: a twenty-seven-year-old interior decorator. After attending college eight hours away from home, Melanie moved even farther away from her support system, moving within a few years from Texas to Las Vegas. Always somewhat of a social butterfly, Melanie couldn't help the feelings of loneliness in this new town. Although she was surrounded by bright lights, tons of excitement, and endless entertainment, Melanie had no one to share her life with. Everyone around her scurried through the weekdays in order to live the party life on the weekends. She began to miss simple things like having friends to chat with over coffee on a Saturday afternoon. The thought of her mother's homemade chicken soup was enough to make her want to pack up and drive the sixteen hours back to Texas. But Melanie's job, her passion for working with fabrics, color, and helping people make their houses into homes, was enough to stick it out in Las Vegas. After a month or so of feeling sorry for herself, Melanie realized that this time out on her own in the desert of Nevada was a great opportunity to strengthen her faith and develop a deeper relationship with God.

Girlfriend Case Study #2

Sarah (Me): a nervous twenty-two-year-old moving into her own place. The biggest stressors of living out on my own were questions like, *Will I be able to financially support myself? What do I do about grown-up things like how to find the best health insurance? How do I pay my taxes? What do I do if my car breaks down?* Though I looked forward to the autonomy of living on my own, what if I failed miserably? These stressful thoughts kept me up at night as I freaked out about the fact that I could and should no longer rely on my parents to handle these real-life issues.

 ## Girlfriend Case Study #3

Jillian: a junior in college who recently turned twenty-one. Jillian is from a family that loves the Lord and sets strict rules for her and her three siblings. A little bit of a rebel at heart, Jillian was the one in her family who would walk right up to that boundary and test it with things like hidden tattoos and a sense of fashion that made her mom, who had a conservative fashion sense, shake her head. But, no matter what, Jillian honored her parents and followed the rules. Turning twenty-one and stepping into adulthood, with the new freedom to go to bars and actually partake, caused Jillian to appreciate the foundation her parents had laid out for her. Jillian stood on that foundation of values, developed her own personal boundaries, and learned to live as an adult who knows how to have a good time without going over the line.

Journal 1
IDENTIFY YOURSELF

• Can you identify with any aspects of the girlfriend case studies? If so, what resonates with you?

_____

_____

_____

_____

• What gets you most excited about the thought of being out on your own?

_____

_____

_____

_____

• What fears or concerns do you have about being out on your own?

_____

_____

_____

_____

_____

Worshiping at the Throne of the King

As Melanie sat alone in her apartment, which she had not yet decorated due to a full load at work, she felt the safety net (her friends and family back home in Texas) ripping out from underneath her, string by string. Melanie sensed that this season of loneliness would open her up to a level of maturity that she wasn't sure she wanted to dive into. Living in a big town and knowing almost no one frightened her a bit. One night, just before she turned out the light, Melanie flipped to the last page marked in her copy of the devotional *Jesus Calling*. Her heart beat fast and the hair on her arm stood up as she realized that the Lord was speaking to her through the words in this little orange devotional book.

> In closeness to Me, you are safe. In the intimacy of My Presence, you are energized. No matter where you are in the world, you know you belong when you sense my nearness . . . I designed you for close communication with your Creator.[8]

Melanie decided that she would now look at her present circumstances and her lack of a support system as a way to grow closer and more dependent on God. She didn't have many distractions, other than her favorite TV show, to keep her from sitting right at the throne of her King and worshiping Him with her full-on trust and dependence. She didn't have someone to run to right away when her car broke down or when she questioned a line item on her bank statement. There was no one to turn to but her Lord, her Hiding Place. This was a very good thing.

Approaching the throne of our King, our Hiding Place, in full-on trust that He is our protection and ultimate guidance is true worship. To give us a better picture of this characteristic of God—our Hiding Place—we can look at a few synonyms of "our Hiding Place": our security, our rock, our sanctuary, our safety. This description of God makes me picture a soft place to find comfort and security when I'm fearful of the unknown. When we step out on our own, so much responsibility is now in our hands that it is easy to let fear and anxiety trap us. Even Jesus needed the comforting presence of His Father, His Hiding Place, when he would steal away from the crowds early in the morning to pray and just be with God.

I love how David worshiped God with his words in Psalm 32. David declared his trust in his Hiding Place in all life situations. When David's life was just peachy, He praised and trusted God. When David's enemies were after him, he still praised and trusted his Hiding Place.

> You are my hiding place; You shall preserve me from trouble; You shall surround me with songs of deliverance. (Psalm 32:7)

Though you and I might not have a king of Israel, sword in hand, ready to have our heads, there are plenty of scary things in this big world to keep us afraid. Whether it is the intimidation of returning home to an empty apartment after a long day or the stress of not knowing where the money will come from for your next trip to the grocery store, your Hiding Place, Jesus, will sweep you up in His strong arms and gently lead you to safety. But it takes initiative on our part to step up to the throne and into His loving protection. Trying to handle our fears alone will keep us in that state of independence wherein we miss out on the true personal growth and maturity that dependence on Him guarantees.

Praising God with the knowledge that, although you are independent from your family, you are never truly alone is music to His ears. A daily approach to our Hiding Place, daily handing over our self-perceived independence, is essential. We discover a weird paradox as we move out on our own: living as Miss Independent but clinging ever so dependently on the Lord. A sense of freedom fills us as we grow into our own faith and our sense of identity in Him, outside of even the grand foundation that our family sets for us as we grow. It might be a terrifying leap out of our safety nets, but this leap gratifies the deep desire to hold tightly to the One who covers all of our fears and anxieties that might bubble up when stepping out on our own.

Use the journal space below to commune with your King in trust and worship that He is your safe Hiding Place. Let the Lord show you through His Word the areas that He will protect you and keep you. Pray through these scriptures to enlighten areas in your life where you are intimidated and anxious about living out on your own. Sometimes we push these fears aside and don't deal with them, never allowing God to step in and show off His power. I'm excited for you to discover more about yourself and your Hiding Place through this chapter.

Journal 1
I WORSHIP AT THE THRONE

• Define your safety net or your support system. Who do you depend on for guidance and protection?

_____

_____

_____

_____

• Do you think this safety net hampers you at all from achieving all-out dependence on God? If so, how?

_____

_____

_____

_____

• How do you think the move to step out on your own in the world can grow your faith in the Lord?

_____

_____

_____

_____

_____

- Flip to the concordance in your Bible and look up a few of these words: *trust, refuge, strong, shepherd.* Write out one or two verses that speak to you.

- What is one way, based on those scriptures, that you can worship your King, your Hiding Place, today?

179

Waiting at the Throne of the King

I remember the first time I realized that the oil in my car didn't magically change itself and that there are responsible actions I must take in order to keep the car running. Once I left home and didn't have my dad to run the car over to the neighborhood mechanic for me, a veil lifted off of my eyes and whoa, did a reality check set in. It never occurred to me all of the grown-up decisions that were required of me to live this life as Miss Independent. Suddenly questions about how to do grown-up life swirled around me, and all I wanted to do was crawl into my bed and hold my childhood blankie. I thought, *How in the world am I to figure all of this out on my own? What if I royally screw up on my taxes and the government comes after me? What if I pick the wrong health insurance and I contract an awful illness that the insurance won't cover? What if someone robs my apartment or I have a fire; how do I figure out renter's insurance? What if . . . what if . . . what if . . .*

I call these items of concern Life Mechanics. These are the nuts and bolts of everyday living that we all must buck up and take care of. These things are not fun to think about, I know. Trust me, I would rather play with my paints and crafty materials than balance my checkbook; but it must be done. There was a time, in fact, when I flat-out ignored the life mechanics and found myself in a sticky situation with a bill collector because I neglected to pay a very small fee for a trip to the urgent care during a bout of strep throat. Another time, denial about being a grown-up set in, and mounds of bills and important bank statements piled up, literally, on my dining room table. We are talking stacks and stacks and stacks of envelopes. I slipped into a state where the responsibilities piled up so high that an overwhelming sense of helplessness kept me from handling the everyday life mechanics of my bank account. Thankfully my mom stepped in and helped me sort through the pile and explore my reasons for not properly handling my newly found grownup Life Mechanics.

It all goes back to fear, intimidation, and anxiety. Do you experience a pure lockdown of all rational behavior when you fear? Are you intimidated by your Life Mechanics? Are you anxious about how to handle it all on your own? Waiting at the throne of our King, our Hiding Place, means we take even the mundane Life Mechanics straight to Him. When I am tempted to curl up and throw the covers over my head because I can't handle the stress of being a grown-up, I've learned that the more productive action is to curl up at the throne of my King and wrap myself in the soft blanket of His wisdom. This soft blanket comes with action on my part, though. I can't just wrap myself up and hide away in ignorance; I must take action and actively trust Him and bring my fears to my Hiding Place. The ability to do this built up over time through prayer.

> Don't be anxious about things; instead, pray. Pray about everything. *He longs to hear your requests*, so talk to God about your needs and be thankful for *what has come*. And know that the peace of God (*a peace* that is beyond any and all of our *human* understanding) will stand watch over your hearts and minds in Jesus, the Anointed One. (Philippians 4:6–7 THE VOICE)

At the throne of my King, our Hiding Place, amidst stress and uncertainty, let us pray without ceasing. Let us not think that anything is out of His control or concern. Let us always see God as the One who cares about even our trivial questions about grown-up life. When we don't bring the Life Mechanics to the throne and wait on Him for direction, we miss out on perfect illumination of how to navigate life. We miss out on little details that could affect us later in life. God protects even things like our financial credit, our decisions over which house to purchase so we don't end up in major debt, the fine details of our 401(k) retirement account that is so crucial for our future. Nothing is beyond His hand and power. Allow your King to sweep up into the Hiding Place all of the minute details of grown-up life, wiping away your stress so you are free to really live life in your newfound dependence on Him.

The journal space below is an opportunity to sort through the list of Life Mechanics that may be stressing you out right now. If you are feeling stressed about these things, let the Lord know about it! He wants to hear you whine and cry like I did when I could no longer handle the pile of papers on my table. But we can't whine, cry, and crawl into our beds in fear if we want His help. We must do the grown-up thing and acknowledge where we need help and lay it before Him—trusting that our King will guide us in our next steps. This journal below might not be the most fun to work through, but there is joy and relief when we get real about the grown-up stuff that seems out of our control.

Journal 3

I WAIT AT THE THRONE OF MY KING

- Below, make a list of Life Mechanics that stress you out. (For example: car insurance, bills, how to buy a house, etc.) Leave two lines between each item on your list. We'll fill them in in a second.

- Under each item in the above list, write exactly what stresses you out about it.

- Take a look at Psalm 32 again. Early on in the chapter we looked at verse 7. Now read one verse further and soak in Psalm 32:8. On the final blank line beneath each Life Mechanic in your list, write a short prayer asking God to guide and direct you in this issue.

- In this chapter we also looked at Philippians 4:6–7. Read this passage again, this time in your own Bible, but start with verse 5. How do you think an attitude of joy and thanksgiving along with prayer affects your outlook on your Life Mechanics and potential stress?

Finding Focus on Him Alone

I sat at a table with a bunch of sweet younger girlfriends, including my friend Jillian. We talked about their struggles as 20-somethings in regard to going out with their friends. Naturally, the topic turned to drinking, which piqued my interest, since this is such a hot topic no matter what age you are. The question at hand was, *How much do I allow myself to drink, if I do drink at all? And how do I handle this now that I'm above the legal drinking age, out from under my parents' wings, free to make my own personal choices on this matter?*

I admitted to my friends that I too have struggled with this question and I understand the plight they are in. I also respect the fact that they care enough about living in a manner that pleases God to even ask these tough questions and analyze their own behavior. Maybe you have asked yourself these same questions.

Though I do not claim to know the answer to this dilemma, I would like to offer up my thoughts and hopefully drum up a meaningful conversation around this topic. Please note: this is not a discussion about whether or not it is biblical to drink alcohol. Rather, it is a discussion on . . .

Boundaries.

Our parents used to set boundaries.

The law sets boundaries.

The Bible sets boundaries.

But what about the boundaries we set for ourselves now that we are mature enough to make our own decisions? There is a plethora of scripture that covers the topic of drunkenness, but the topic of drinking in general is a bit gray in my opinion. Since I am a black-and-white type of person, gray areas make my head spin. I like to have lists of "do this but don't do that." What do you think about this set of scriptures to work off of as we form our personal boundaries on drinking?

A mind focused on the flesh is doomed to death, but a mind focused on the Spirit will find full life and complete peace. You see, a mind focused on the flesh is declaring war against God; it defies the authority of God's law and is incapable of following His path. So it *is clear that* God takes no pleasure in those who live oriented to the flesh. (Romans 8:6–8 THE VOICE)

So how can we know what it looks like to have a mind set on the Spirit when we are out with our friends and alcohol is involved? Turn to Galatians 5 and look at the fruit of the Spirit. If we are doing anything in life—not just drinking—that keeps us from living out the fruit of the Spirit, God is displeased.

Here are the fruit of the Spirit to use as a guideline for setting boundaries in our life:

Love, joy, peace, patience, kindness, goodness, faithfulness, gentleness, self-control. (Galatians 5:22 paraphrased)

What if the boundaries we set for ourselves looked like this: Anytime alcohol is involved and we partake, if the fruit of the Spirit are not evident in our actions, thoughts, and words, our boundary has been pushed, and this does not please God. We then know we need to pull back. The cool thing about this thought process is that we can set boundaries based on our need to exude the fruit of the Spirit at all times. So if alcohol is involved, we know when to pull back based on how present the fruit of the Spirit is in our thoughts and actions while drinking.

We can apply this to other parts of life too.

- ❧ Eating
- ❧ Working
- ❧ Exercising
- ❧ Shopping
- ❧ Conversations with friends

We need boundaries in all areas of our lives, don't we? If we are obsessed with going to the gym so much so that we lose peace about our self-worth, a boundary has been crossed. If we work so much that joy is lost, a boundary has been crossed. If we drink too much and self-control goes out the window, a boundary has absolutely been crossed.

The beauty of focusing on Jesus is that when we mess up and cross the boundaries, He is still there, with open arms waiting for us to walk back into our Hiding Place with a heart that says, "I'm sorry, Lord, I messed up big-time. Help me reset my boundaries so I can please You." When we are mature enough to acknowledge that we've messed up, there is an open door for personal growth. If we refocus ourselves on that biblical foundation, allow Him to pick us back up and dust us off, and keep going with life, we're better for it if we've truly learned our lesson. The Hiding Place that God welcomes us back into has room for us, even after we've crossed our boundaries.

Journal 4

I FIND FOCUS ON HIM ALONE

• What benefits do you see in setting personal boundaries in your life? In addition to pleasing God, how do you see boundaries as helpful to living a full life? See Romans 8:6–8 on page 186.

_____

_____

_____

_____

_____

_____

• What boundaries have you set in your life when it comes to things like drinking, spending money, working, etc.?

_____

_____

_____

_____

_____

_____

_____

• Are there any personal boundaries that you need to establish in light of setting your focus on the King?

• Journal through the concept of the fruit of the Spirit (Galatians 5:22) as a tried and true guideline of how to set personal boundaries. What are some ways you've exhibited the fruit of the Spirit as you've lived within your boundaries?

Stress Diverted

The journey through life as Miss Independent, fully dependent on your King, will not be without bumps and mess-ups and cleanups. Too often we pretend as if we know all the answers so we don't have to depend on anyone for direction when we step out on our own into a grown-up life. The misconception that you have to know it all in order to live on your own blocks us from the meaningful experience of personal growth. Our King offers a wealth of wisdom in every area of life, even our Life Mechanics. Too often we think the concepts of the Bible don't apply to the mundane details of our day, but they do! Though the Bible doesn't directly address how to fix a discrepancy in our checkbook, it does give us encouragement to live life responsibly and with integrity. When we need direction on how to handle a disagreement with our coworker without causing a ruckus at our cubicle, the Word leads us to an attitude of humility and understanding. All of our Life Mechanics are addressed when we make ourselves available in the Hiding Place, at the throne of our King, with an open mind and a need for His perfect wisdom.

Psalm 139:7–12 (THE VOICE) will lead us to grasp just what our Hiding Place, our King, has to offer when we worship, wait, and focus at the throne.

> Can I go anywhere apart from Your Spirit? Is there anywhere I can go to escape Your *watchful* presence? If I go up into heaven, You are there. If I make my bed in the realm of the dead, You are there. If I ride on the wings of morning, if I make my home in the most isolated part of the ocean, Even then You will be there to guide me; Your right hand will embrace me, *for You are always there.* Even if I *am afraid and* think *to myself,* "There is no doubt that the darkness will swallow me, the light around me will soon be turned to night," *You can see* in the dark, for it is not dark to Your eyes.

Journal 5

I LAY IT ALL DOWN BEFORE THE THRONE

Below are some prayer point journal prompts. Finish these thoughts with your own words in a written prayer.

* *Father God, show me the peace and comfort I so desperately desire from Your Hiding Place . . .*

_____

_____

* *Lord, lead me in the way to your presence every day, for I don't always know how to make my way into Your Hiding Place . . .*

_____

_____

* *I commit to You, my King, my independence. These are the things in my life that I know I must hand over to You for guidance and direction . . .*

_____

_____

_____

* *I thank You, Father, in advance for the ways You will grow me and stretch me as I live out on my own . . .*

_____

_____

_____

*Go to **www.liveitoutblog.com/stress-point** to watch a video from Sarah on this chapter's Stress Point!*

CHAPTER 9

STRESS POINT:
MAKING A DIFFERENCE
I CAN MAKE A DIFFERENCE
(START A RIPPLE)

Do you ever find yourself longing to leave your mark on the world? To effect change or impart hope in your surroundings? Because women are made with compassionate hearts, most of us have an innate ability to zero in on the great need and depravity in our world. The problem is that we often recognize the magnitude of that very need and feel paralyzed because we think there is no way we, as a individuals, can possibly do anything to change the situation. Some of us see the need and don't even know where to begin. Some of us see the need and think that there is no true way to make an impact. Some of us see the need and think we have nothing to offer. I hope that this chapter encourages you in your effort to make a difference in *your* world, in your immediate sphere of influence. It just takes small, meaningful strides to start a ripple effect that changes hearts and shows people the love of Jesus.

Girlfriend Case Study #1

Eugenia "Skeeter" Phelan from the book-turned-movie *The Help*. Set in the Deep South in the 1960s, the story's main character, Skeeter, a recent college graduate from the University of Mississippi, or "Ole Miss," dreams of one day writing important stories for a major publication in New York City. After Skeeter moves back home to take a job as a columnist for the local paper in Jackson, Mississippi, she attempts to fit in with her old hometown crowd of affluent southern belles who are waited on by their longtime African-American maids. Skeeter is appalled by how her friends treat these maids, though her friends know nothing different than the all-powerful Jim Crow racial segregation laws. The wonderfully idealistic Skeeter sets out to interview a dozen maids and write an anonymous book about how they are treated as second- and even third-class citizens by their white employers. The threat of retribution from the Ku Klux Klan is real, yet Skeeter is determined to shed light on the desperate plight of the African-American community in Jackson. She struggles in the face of difficult questions: *Should she leave the topic alone? Does she dare face being socially ostracized? Or, should she give hope to the beautiful women—the maids—who have loved the families they've worked for and raised their children, yet face terrible, demeaning treatment?*

Girlfriend Case Study #2

Sarah (Me again!): a dreamer of grand plans. I love nothing more than the thrill of brainstorming a new endeavor, and I jump in with both feet every time. These grand plans are often amazing, fabulous, exciting schemes I plan on implementing for Jesus. Sometimes these plans include a mission project I propose to my church leadership. Sometimes these plans include a new social media campaign for the ministry I write for. Sometimes these grand plans are for a bridal shower for a friend, and although I know it should be a low-key affair, it turns into an all-out bash. I ponder while I drive; I plan out the fine details, and then . . . I fizzle out. The adrenaline rush from the passion about my new idea turns into stress because I've taken on a new endeavor that I can't handle on my own—one I may or may not have been completely prayed through. This is where I go wrong.

 ### Girlfriend Case Study #3

Blakely: a young, compassionate 20-something working as an administrative assistant at a nonprofit organization. When Blakely was a young girl, God spoke to her heart and planted a seed that would soon blossom into a sweet desire to impact the lives of people around her. As Blakely sits at her desk, filing paperwork and emailing potential donors, she wonders when the Lord will give her the opportunity to really shake things up, to do something worthwhile. After work, she drives through a fast-food restaurant to pick up a quick dinner on the run, since the youth group she leads begins soon. Flipping the station on her iPhone Pandora app, Blakely hears the bluesy pop song "Waiting on the World to Change" by John Mayer, and her heart bursts. *Lord, I'm here. I want to change the world. Just give me the opportunity. I'm ready!*

Journal 1

IDENTIFY YOURSELF

• Which one of these case studies do you identify with most?

I think I identify the most with case studies #1 & #3. I feel ready at times, but feelings of fear of being socially ostracized or that I don't know enough hinders my growth in making a difference.

• Where do you see need in the world as a whole?

_____

_____

_____

• If you have a desire to make a difference in the world, write out how you dream of doing that. Then write out your frustrations. What is it that is keeping you from making a difference? Or, are you frustrated with the state of the world in general and feel overwhelmed that you, one person, might not be able to make a dent of change?

_____

_____

_____

_____

Worshiping at the Throne of the King

In our quest to make a difference in the world, we run into the questions, *how do I not waste my life? How do I avoid spending my days sitting around doing nothing and make my life count for something?* As I asked myself those very questions, John Piper's book *Don't Waste Your Life* gave me a renewed passion for worship. I like things simplified into statements I can easily wrap my brain around and replay over and over, and John Piper made a statement in his book that is simple yet transformational. See if this statement gets you all fired up as it did me several years ago.

> The opposite of wasting your life is to live by a single, soul-satisfying passion for the supremacy of God in all things.[9]

This single, soul-satisfying passion begins with connecting the supremacy of God and the enormity of what Jesus did on the cross of Calvary. We then allow those two realities to permeate every area of life, including our desire to make a difference in the world. With each of the stress points we discuss in this book, we draw back to a worship of our King of Kings, recognizing that He is the center of our life issues. It is no different with our desire to change the world.

As I've learned over the last year, my grand plans to do great things for God fall flat if I think that I can dream and plan and then expect God to graciously join in and bless me. A major paradigm shift occurred when I realized that God is already doing amazing things around me. If I take some time to ask Him to reveal an area where He is moving and shaking things up, then and only then can I join in with my God-given talents and affect change. Jesus serves as the perfect example when He says,

My Father has been working until now, and I have been working. . . .
Most assuredly, I say to you, the Son can do nothing of Himself, but
what He sees the Father do; for whatever He does, the Son also
does in like manner. For the Father loves the Son, and shows Him all
things that He Himself does; and He will show Him greater works
than these, that you may marvel. (John 5:17, 19–20)

If you are like me, you may be thinking, *Whoa, whoa, whoa! You mean I
can't come up with fanciful dreams and expect God to grant them at my beck
and call? You mean I can't plan out my life or projects and pray God's will over
them? Huh?*

After I got over the initial shock in this new thought process, I searched
for a way to visualize this new concept. When we have determined that
we desire to follow Jesus and His plans, it is as if we are stepping onto a
subway. We have to physically go to that subway station, hop on a train,
and join in on its predetermined journey. This is what it looks like to join in
on what God is already doing.

The opposite of taking the subway is when we plan out a place we
desire to visit, call a taxi, the taxi comes to us, and we tell the taxi where
to drive. Are you catching my drift here?

I have found myself walking through these two scenarios every time I
feel a nudge of a new brainstorm or a new plan brewing. I used to come
up with these fanciful plans of wonderful, noble things I would do for God
and then call up my taxi to take me there. Yes, those plans would pan out
some or most of the time. But I have to wonder: would my grand plans
be more impactful had I just made my way to the subway and joined in
on what God was already doing? Would things have gone more smoothly
if I had prayed for the Lord to show me ways He was moving around me
and prayed for the doors of that subway to open so I could join in with my
God-given talents?

If Jesus followed this way of thinking as He states in John 5, I sure as
heck better follow it too, right?

Getting back to the single-minded passion and worship of the supreme King, the first way to jump on His already moving subway and let Him use us to make a difference is to connect people with the reality of the cross. When Jesus allowed Himself to be beaten, mocked, and hung on the cross that one fateful Friday, He bridged the gap between us and God to eliminate our sin, move us away from the consequences of our sin, and allow us to live in the everlasting peace and love of our God. Jesus provided the way for us to change our destructive ways and gave us the first step to helping those who are in need. Because He conquered death and rose to sit on His throne for eternity, we all have victory over life's junk.

What God is already doing in the world around us—the route of His subway—is already determined, and the journey began with Jesus and the cross. God provided the first step in effecting change. One name of the Lord that I like to connect to our need to make a difference is *Jehovah-Nissi*, or "The Lord Is My Banner." In times of war, especially in the Old Testament, the soldiers would hold up a banner or a flag to signify just who they were and where their allegiance lay. Throughout the Old Testament, Israel fought enemy after enemy, and with the Lord's help they were victorious. One instance of this is in Exodus 17 where Joshua and Moses were leading the soldiers in a fierce battle with an enemy nation. Moses stood on the top of a hill with a staff of God in hand. All the while Moses lifted this staff, Israel prevailed in the battle. When Moses tired and dropped the staff, the enemy prevailed. In the end, some men helped Moses hold up the staff of God, and Israel won the battle. Though Moses and Joshua were technically the commanders of the army of Israel, it was obvious in this battle that God poured out His power over the army. God won the battle. Moses then built an alter in remembrance of this battle proclaiming, "The LORD is my banner" (Exodus 17:15).

The Hebrew for *Nissi* or *Nes* is sometimes translated to mean a literal pole in which one would hang an insignia. These flags and banners served as a point of focus for the troops to instill hope and focus on the task at hand. Using the name Jehovah-Nissi, we worship in the fact that God is our ultimate focal point.

He goes before us, as Jesus did on the cross, and paves the way for us to live a life of full, unabashed praise and worship at the throne of our King. Our Jehovah-Nissi always provided this path to worship in a powerful way through the blood shed by Jesus and by raising Christ from the dead to sit at the throne. Jehovah-Nissi doesn't only provide for us as believers to make a difference by telling people about the cross, but He gives true relief to those people in need when they accept Jesus as their Savior. Jesus did all the work; we just need to join in and spread the word as we choose actions to take while serving others. We will discuss in greater detail some practical actions to take in the next section.

First, the cross . . . then the action on our part.

First, the single mother with two young kids needs to see that Jesus sees her lonely heart . . . then she needs our help.

First, the homeless teenage girl addicted to meth needs to know that Jesus has the power to bring her out of the gutter of dark and painful memories . . . then she needs our help to bring her out of the physical gutter.

First, the child with leukemia needs to know that he has a hope and future because Jesus died on the cross . . . then he needs us to bring him laughter and relief from the pain of his disease.

Our Jehovah-Nissi first provides a way back to Him through the cross. He then gives us guidance on showing others how they, too, can worship at the throne. A pure, passionate, single-minded worship begins with coming before the King, praising Him for bringing us out of the pit, then sharing that good news and physically taking action with those in need.

Journal 2
I WILL WORSHIP AT THE THRONE

Let's explore a bit deeper the name of the Lord, Jehovah-Nissi, in regards to our quest to join in where God is doing His thing rather than planning and scheming our own grand plans. Jehovah-Nissi, The Lord Is My Banner, gives us a clear picture of lifting up our banner, our worship, our praise, our recognition—making Him famous and flying His flag. By worshiping Jehovah-Nissi, we take the stance that He is due all the credit and worship for the work of the cross. When we acknowledge this we stop living in the illusion that we can do great things in the world on our own.

• An example of how God equips us to praise and worship Him is in the "banner" of Psalm 60:4–5:

> You have given a banner to those who fear You,
> That it may be displayed because of the truth.
> That Your beloved may be delivered,
> Save with Your right hand, and hear me.

• God has given us a standard to live by based on the cross, and a flag to fly that praises His name rather than our own; therefore, those who fear Him, those who show reverence to the King, take part in displaying His truth. In your own words, write out how you would display the truth. How would you talk to someone in need about the cross?

_____

_____

_____

_____

_____

- Read Psalm 20:5 (THE VOICE):

  When you win, *we will not be silent!* We will shout and raise high our banners in the great name of our God! May the Eternal say yes to all your requests.

- Take a few moments to "not be silent," and write out a prayer of thanksgiving and praise to your Jehovah-Nissi, your Banner.

Waiting at the Throne of the King

What I love about Blakely is her compassion and her willingness to see the need around her through a prayerful heart. It would be tempting to let the pictures of starving children in Africa or news stories of earthquake-ravaged Japan make us throw up our hands in helpless surrender. Though the need is great in the world at large, there are people in our own backyards who could use a helping hand and the hope of our King.

Did you notice in the girlfriend case study where Blakely cried out to the Lord in frustration that she thought she wasn't doing enough to make a difference? All the while, she pleaded to God as she drove to teach Bible study to a group of sweet yet insecure thirteen-year-olds who desperately need to hear that they are beautiful the way God made them and that the mean girls don't define who they are. Blakely makes a difference every single week when she pours out her energy and love on these girls and leads them in Bible study. This is her backyard. Though mission trips to Africa are so very needed (please hear me say that), we don't have to take long trips abroad to feel like we joined in on changing the world. All it takes is opening our eyes to the needs of our community—in our own backyard—and prayerfully asking God where He is already moving. We wait at the throne of our King for Him to shine light on the darkness in our immediate sphere of influence.

In the book of Matthew, Jesus teaches that one day we will all be gathered around the throne of the King and split up into two groups based on whether we followed Jesus as our Savior or if we denied His Kingship. Though our good deeds alone do not qualify us to spend eternity in heaven, they are tangible pieces of evidence that we are followers of Christ. Because we love Him, we love His creation and His people; therefore, we desire to serve Jesus by serving others. In Matthew, Jesus said to those who had faithfully served Him:

Then the King will say to those on His right hand, "Come, you blessed of My Father, inherit the kingdom prepared for you from the foundation of the world: for I was hungry and you gave Me food; I was thirsty and you gave Me drink; I was a stranger and you took Me in; I was naked and you clothed Me; I was sick and you visited Me; I was in prison and you came to Me." (Matthew 25:34–36)

Jesus' followers proceeded to ask just who these people were that they served. It's as if they reached out to those in need around them, showed love to the people in their community, and served them as if it were no big deal, just part of their everyday routine. Jesus answered His followers' question with this statement: "Assuredly, I say to you, inasmuch as you did it to one of the least of these My brethren, you did it to Me" (Matthew 25:40).

It warms my heart how these followers approached their daily lives with time to break from their tasks to stop and serve someone else in need. They truly made a difference in their world and served their King at the same time. Who is in your own backyard? Is there someone you pass by, day in and day out, on the way to work or during your daily jog, who needs to know that in Christ, they can conquer the pit that swallowed them whole? Who is it that needs a sweet smile from you or a warm blanket as a sign that God sees their need?

Here are some examples of ways that you can clothe, feed, visit, and encourage those in your community:

- ❧ A local nonprofit group is "stuffing the bus" and collecting supplies to give sweet little underprivileged grade-schoolers brand new backpacks full of loot for their first day of school. *Do you see Jesus in the eyes of this child who is too embarrassed to tell the teacher he doesn't have a pencil to perform his math assignment?*

- ❧ The battered women's shelter across town needs a fresh coat of paint to make the house a home. *Do you see Jesus in the hollowness of the battered and bruised hearts of these women who need a safe refuge both physically and spiritually?*

- ❧ Your elderly neighbor is sweating bullets trying to pull up the weeds in her special garden on a hot summer day. *Do you see Jesus in a small act of bring her a glass of iced tea and letting her sit in the shade while you trim her rose bushes?*

- ❧ Your thing is fashion, and the local high school started a program to help the low-income kids dress professionally in order to prepare for college scholarship interviews. *Do you see Jesus in the need of that sweet senior in high school who dreams of a college degree so she can later make more money to support her family?*

- ❧ The military wives small group at your church is looking for some babysitters so the moms can have a girl's night out sans kids. *Do you see Jesus in the need to relieve the mother's stress as she cares for her three small children all the while worrying about the safety of her deployed soldier/husband?*

You see, one small act of kindness can effect big change. Like a tiny pebble that, when thrown into the water, starts a small ripple that eventually spreads throughout the entire pond, by committing our time, talents, and even money, we set in motion a ripple of change in our own back yard.

- ❧ That child in need of school supplies goes on, years later, to win a merit scholarship in mathematics. He makes his way to Harvard and later forges new ground in pharmaceutical research.

- ❧ A woman who ends up at the battered women's shelter later finds a job and rents a house so that her kids no longer live in fear.

- ❧ Your elderly neighbor's garden grows beautifully, and she is able to bless her friends and family on their birthdays with gifts of blossoming roses.

⋒ The high school senior gets a boost of self-esteem through your advice and encouragement and has a successful freshman year at college, all expenses paid by a prestigious scholarship.

⋒ The military wife is able to take a deep breath, relax, and regroup in order to live life to the fullest while her husband is deployed oversees.

When I sat down for coffee to touch base with Blakely, she expressed her excitement over how and when God is using her to make a difference in her community. She said, "God has really challenged me lately to make a difference right where He has me at this moment instead of me planning how I will make a difference once I'm somewhere else."

Where does God have you at this moment? Will you prayerfully approach the throne of the King, your Jehovah-Nissi, with an open heart and alert eyes to see the sick, the lonely, the thirsty, the hungry? Will you feed them, visit them, give them a drink of water as if you were serving Jesus?

Journal 3
I WAIT AT THE THRONE OF MY KING

• After reading the section on waiting at the throne of the King in regard to making a difference in the world, how would you define the term *waiting*? For example, would it mean prayerfully asking God to show you where He wants you to make a difference?

_____

_____

_____

_____

• In your Bible, look up John 15:1–5 and read through it a couple of times. Write out verse 5 in the journal space below. In the New King James Version, the word *abides* is used: "He who abides in Me, and I in him . . ." What word is used in the translation you use?

_____

_____

_____

_____

_____

- The word *abide* means to remain, stay, dwell, endure. The word *fruit* in this passage brings to mind the fruit of the Spirit (Galatians 5): love, joy, peace, patience, kindness, goodness, faithfulness, gentleness, and self-control. By continuously remaining connected with Jesus (abiding), your fruit (love, joy, peace, patience, etc.) will be poured out on those around you. How does this apply to serving others and making a difference in your own backyard?

_____

_____

_____

_____

- Take a few minutes to prayerfully brainstorm how you can make a difference in your community—your backyard. Feel free to use my suggestions above as a starting point! Write down your ideas here. Only brainstorm about two to three ideas. Make this list manageable, and include things you can accomplish in the next several months.

_____

_____

_____

_____

Finding Focusing on Him Alone

I just completed a hardcore workout video by Jillian Michaels, who said something that stopped me right in my tracks in the transition between the Warrior I and Downward Dog yoga poses. How much does this quote apply to our topic at hand?

> *"I want you to get comfortable with being uncomfortable."*

Though Jillian is referring to the grueling act of transforming our bodies via exercise, getting comfortable with the feeling of discomfort applies to our spiritual transformation when we serve our King by serving others. Skeeter busted out of her own comfort zone when she decided to secretly write the book that would make a dent in racism in Jackson, Mississippi. It took a single-minded focus on the end goal for Skeeter to travel across town, where whites usually didn't set foot, to spend hours interviewing the maids and writing their stories—the good, the bad, and the very ugly. It took a laser-sharp conviction that what she planned on publishing would make a difference in the South. Skeeter had to get comfortable with discomfort.

Sometimes we see the need in our own backyard and think we are not equipped to help. Maybe you are intimidated by the thought of speaking to people you don't know personally, so you shy away from projects like visiting the local nursing home. Or, maybe you feel uncomfortable etching out time in your week to go paint the women's shelter on Saturday morning after working a full forty hours. Jillian says in another of her workout videos that true change happens within us when stuff hurts and we want to quit. Whether it hurts to break out of our routine to paint, or to break out of our insecurities to give someone hope and encouragement, something in us transforms when we take the steps and move through our discomfort. Something deep down in our soul realizes that when we walk through that discomfort, a refinement occurs that cuts away our self-focus.

> You should greatly rejoice *in what is waiting for you*, even if now for a little while you have to suffer various trials. *Suffering tests* your faith which is more valuable than gold (remember that gold, although it is perishable, is tested by fire) so that if it is found genuine, you can receive praise, honor, and glory when Jesus the Anointed, *our Liberating King*, is revealed at last. (I Peter 1:6-7 THE VOICE)

Just as gold is purified in fire, our faith and our character is purified when we serve others and strive to make a difference, regardless of our level of comfort or convenience. The only way to gain the courage to serve and get out of our comfort zone is through a single-minded focus on why we want to make a difference in our world. Have you ever asked yourself just what your motivation is? Maybe you aren't quite certain of your motivation, just certain that you need to do something. If this is the case, refer with me back to Matthew 25 where Jesus says that He is blessed and glorified when we reach out to others. Long-lasting motivation to make a difference should stem from our heart, which longs to make Jesus known and lifted up in the ways we serve others.

- ∝ **Discomfort**: You would rather stay in bed on Saturday morning than help paint a fresh coat on the building of the women's shelter.

- ∝ **Refinement**: That Saturday, you experience a sweet sense of joy in the crisp early morning hours as you spend time with your friends, not only brushing paint on a house but painting the hearts of hurt women with a fresh coat of hope.

- ∝ **Discomfort**: You would much rather put your extra money toward the purchase of those super-cute Steve Madden heels than buy extra school supplies to "stuff the bus."

- ∝ **Refinement**: By giving away your money, there is a freedom in knowing that happiness doesn't come from buying stuff.

☙ **Discomfort**: It is hard for you to schedule time in your busy workday to head over to the local high school to mentor a sweet young student on how to put her best foot forward for college interviews.

☙ **Refinement**: You realize that you have a knack for relating to young girls, and you enjoy using what you've learned about the "real world" to give her advice on college preparation. Maybe you even volunteer your time more often for a mentoring program?

Just as we enjoy the benefits of our physical transformations when we exercise like mad, regardless of the pain, we also enjoy the spiritual benefits when we focus on our King and allow Him to use us to change lives in our own backyard. There is nothing like the feeling of joy, peace, or hope Jesus pours over us when we impart those very same things on others. Will you join me in getting comfortable with being uncomfortable for the sake of making Jesus known to those in our own backyard?

Journal 4
I FIND MY FOCUS ON HIM ALONE

• What is your motivation when brainstorming and thinking critically about how you can make a difference?

_____

_____

_____

• Let's revisit Matthew 25, this time focusing on verses 31–44. Take a few moments to read these verses in your own Bible and soak in the stark difference between the two groups described in this passage: those who didn't serve others and those who did. Write in your own words the consequences for those who love Jesus as their Savior _and_ serve others. Then, write in your own words the consequences for those who might say they love Jesus, yet neglect the need in their own backyard.

_____

_____

_____

_____

_____

_____

_____

- What is your present level of discomfort? What objections or excuses pop up when the thoughts cross your mind regarding serving others? Let's get real here. Just be honest and express your thoughts in this private journal.

Stress Diverted

I hope that you find encouragement in the girlfriend stories within this chapter. Just like Skeeter, we make a difference in our world when we recognize a need before us even when making a difference is extremely uncomfortable. With a single-minded focus to worship our Jehovah-Nissi, we can have the courage to get comfortable with being uncomfortable. It is only by pushing ourselves out of our status quo that we live out a refined faith. I hope that you've learned a thing or two from my story about making the mistake of jumping into projects without prayerful consideration of where God is already moving. Consider whether you will take the taxi or the subway. And finally, Blakeley inspires us to simply look in our own backyard to find ways to serve our community. It doesn't have to be complicated; small acts of service add up to lives changed.

Psalm 145 says, "One generation shall praise Your works to another, and shall declare Your mighty acts. I will meditate on the glorious splendor of Your majesty, and on Your wondrous works" (vv. 4–5).

Will you join me and other women in an effort to be the generation that makes a big deal about our King? Making Jesus our Banner—our Jehovah-Nissi—requires more than just lip service. It requires living out the Kingship of Christ and making Him famous through our actions. The world around us needs women who stand for the truth of God's Word and take bold action with loving and caring hearts. You are more than equipped. You are more than prepared. You have so very much to offer. Get out of your comfort zone, get into your backyard, and start that small ripple, girlfriend!

Journal 5

I LAY IT ALL DOWN BEFORE THE THRONE

Below are some prayer point journal prompts. Finish these thoughts with your own words in a written prayer.

- *Lord, You are so very gracious and full of compassion. I will declare Your greatness and mercy to those around me by . . .* (Hint: See Psalm 145:8.)

- *Father, Your kingdom is everlasting and endures through all generations. I want to be a part of the generation that makes Your name famous . . .*

- *Lord, help me to recognize my discomfort in serving others . . .*

- *Jehovah-Nissi, I want my faith refined so I can live it out and glorify You with my actions . . .*

*Go to **www.liveitoutblog.com/stress-point** to watch a video from Sarah on this chapter's Stress Point!*

CHAPTER 19

STRESS POINT:
SPIRITUAL MATURITY

GROWING THROUGH
THE STRESS

Stress is easy to quantify when we are discussing things like money, career, and dating. We hold somewhat concrete images in our minds when fretting or worrying about the prevalent life issues you and I have worked through together in this book. The topic of our spiritual maturity is more elusive and harder to wrap our minds around. I hope that by the time you get to this final chapter you have already approached the throne of your King many times and have experienced a transformation in your view of God and how you live out that view. Life throws curves and twists and turns our way, but when we maneuver our way down the path God has us on with a focused eye on the throne, those curves and twists are more manageable. You might even begin to find joy within life struggles, knowing that the King sees your drama, He hears your pleas, and He is more than able to take the wheel and drive your car down life's hairy roadways. Please forgive me if you now have Carrie Underwood's "Jesus Take the

Wheel" stuck in your head. There could be worse songs to replay in your brain over and over!

I'd like to define the term *spiritual maturity* in order to keep us from thinking it is something unattainable or a label that only studied theologians claim. Some of my most spiritually mature friends are my 20-something girlfriends whose fiery hearts for Jesus and passion to serve Him well qualify them to be labeled "mature" in my book, regardless of their age. For our conversation, let's say that a spiritually mature woman is someone who

- is in continual motion toward the throne of her King.

- has a heart that sees its faults and readily owns up to its mistakes, knowing she is forgiven because Jesus loved her so much He died on the cross for her.

- questions Jesus and evaluates her faith every day with assurance that questions are healthy and acceptable.

- habitually opens her Bible with reverence and desires that the Word of God flow into every area of her life. She never ceases to spend time with Him, and if she does neglect this quality time, she knows she is always welcome right back to the throne.

- loves others more than herself because she knows we are all created and loved by our almighty King.

Does this definition sit well with you? I hope that through this book you have already personally developed some of these qualities. If you feel like you are yet to grow in your faith, no worries. We *all* have room to grow when it comes to believing in Jesus in every stress point of our lives. The fact that you are working through this book and desire to worship your King opens the door for a spiritual maturity that comes with time. But during this growth process, please celebrate the connections you've already made with the Lord and look ahead for new and exciting detours; twists and turns are awaiting you.

Girlfriend Case Study #1

Lilly: a professional ballerina with a sweet spirit and a pure heart for the Lord. Every Wednesday night our young adults group meets. With the lights turned down to alleviate any distractions, our group rocks it out as a few guys pour out their own worship through a full-on rock band. All eyes are turned toward worship of the King. Some raise their hands, some fall to their knees in humble surrender. If you glance to the back of the room you will find sweet Lilly dancing for the Lord. Though not making a show of it, one can't help but look in awe at the communion playing out between Lilly and Jesus. She dances for an audience of One.

 ## Girlfriend Case Study #2

Gina: a twenty-nine-year-old salesperson. Gina is good at her job, but the seven years working her tail off has taken a toll, and complacency threatens her motivation every day. Grumbling and complaining when her boss asks her for extra reports, Gina half-heartedly muddles through the assignment, and before she knows it Gina's attitude affects her team. She never meant to influence her coworkers in such a negative way, and Gina knows that she is definitely not representing Jesus well within her crowd of non-believers at work.

 ## Girlfriend Case Study #3

Sarah (Me): a hard-working girl living a life that was over the top with responsibilities and deadlines at work. After unsuccessfully attempting to exercise in order to alleviate the stress, I decided a glass of wine would do the trick. One glass turned into two, which turned into half a bottle by the time I wobbled to bed. You'd better believe that the cottonmouth and the headache the next morning served as a strong reminder that pouring the wine to wring out stress only added to a guilty conscience the next morning.

Journal 1
IDENTIFY YOURSELF

• Please take a look at our working definition of spiritual maturity or growth. Journal your thoughts about the definition in general as well as how you feel about it in regard to where your faith stands. Does this definition intimidate you? If so, it is okay! This is simply a definition; no one will ever meet each quality all the time. Journal through your thoughts prayerfully.

_____

_____

_____

_____

_____

_____

• Take a look at 1 Peter 1:8 below. We will come back to this scripture later in the chapter, but for now soak in this verse:

Although you haven't seen Jesus, you still love Him. Although you don't yet see Him, you do believe in Him and celebrate with a joy that is glorious and beyond words. (1 Peter 1:8 THE VOICE)

• How does this verse speak to you when it comes to spiritual maturity and our continual movement toward the throne of the King?

• Do you see yourself in any of the girlfriend case studies? If so, how?

Worshiping at the Throne of the King

Some would say that my friend Lilly has an unorthodox method of worship. Some would even scoff at her dancing before the King. But not only is her worship-filled dancing completely biblical (2 Samuel 6:14), it is a pure, unabashed offering focused on the Lord, our *Adonai*. I'm inspired by Lilly's interaction with the Lord to express my own worship of the King in a more meaningful way.

For this final chapter, let's worship our King, our *Adonai*, which translates as "Master." Through this book, the various names of God show us His character and how that character draws us into a deeper relationship with our King. I hope that these names of God have given you a better understanding of just who God is and just who He is to you. This final name of God we'll explore—Adonai, Master—might freak you out. The world tells us that we are the master of our own destiny. That we make our dreams happen; that we hold the key to success in life. Though well-meaning dreamers like to spread this sentiment on greeting cards, with doodles on notebooks, in tweets, or through status updates, this misguided notion locks us into a state where we *think* we are in control of our destiny, our life path, our stress points.

There is freedom when we relent to His control. *Why, you might ask, is there freedom in worshiping our Master? Won't I miss out on the exhilaration of making life decisions for myself?* Why would we feel tied down if we really grasp just who our Master is?

> O Eternal One, our Lord, Your majestic name is heard throughout
> the earth; Your magnificent glory shines far above the skies. (Psalm
> 8:1 THE VOICE)

We will begin to find freedom in this name of the Lord—Adonai, Master—when we worship daily in the freedom of relenting completely to His reign and control over our lives, over all of our stress points. Just as Lilly overtly worshiped her Adonai with dancing, we too can take very personal stances of worship. The freedom to worship with hands raised brings us a body posture that opens our heart to say, *Lord, my Master, I release my life stress to You. I don't care what others think of my outward expressions, You are the One I'm singing to. You alone give me freedom and release from gripping with tight fists the areas of my world that hurt my heart and stress me out.*

Approaching the throne to daily worship the Master means we also rid our heart of pride. I should say, we *attempt* to rid our heart of pride, for pride is one of those heart conditions most difficult to eliminate. But again, as we have journaled together in this book, the holy nature of our God inspires us to put our pride aside even though it is our nature to believe we are in control. One way that I put my own pride aside is to literally bow down before my Master or even lay face down on the floor. I usually do not take this posture in public. These are heartfelt expressions reserved for intimate, quite moments with God in my own house. I release the part of my heart that does not lift my Master up above all and physically remind myself that He is high and lifted up, above all of my life junk. He is greater than what I think I can accomplish on my own.

When we take on humility in worship through our physical stance, we must not feel that our posture is degrading. Because of the innate powerful and mighty nature of our Adonai, when we bow low before Him we're instead lifted high because of our stance within His presence. He reaches down with His masterful arms, lifts us up before His throne, and smiles in our efforts of worship. Jesus delights in our worship of Him in every stress point. In fact, He expects it because He is worthy.

A week before Jesus died on the cross and triumphantly rose from the dead to reign as our King and Master, He rode into Jerusalem while His many disciples heralded and praised their King. This triumphant entry into the holy city displayed on earth what was already true in heaven: that Jesus is King and Lord. Place yourself in the crowds who worshiped Him. *Do you feel the excitement of those who so desperately needed the hope and assurance Jesus offers? Do you understand the enormity of this event? Would* you cry out with the crowds: "Blessed is the King who comes in the name of the Lord! Peace in heaven and glory in the highest!" (Luke 19:38)?

Jesus the King will be worshiped whether we are the ones offering it or not. When the Pharisees, who viewed Jesus as only a teacher rather than King and Adonai, saw the commotion made by those worshiping Jesus as He rode through the city, they insisted that He stop the frenzy unfolding around them. But Jesus knocked down their claim saying, "I tell you that if these should keep silent, the stones would immediately cry out" (Luke 19:40).

The earth is the creation of the Master. The creation knows its Master and will worship Him whether or not we, the most precious aspect of creation, acknowledge and celebrate His reign. I don't know about you, but I don't want leave it up to the stones. I want to participate in the worship that our Master is due.

In our working definition of spiritual maturity, I proposed that growth is defined by a continual motion toward the throne; a daily approach to worship—somehow, someway—by any method that keeps us in constant movement toward our King. As we move toward our King, He stretches us, teaches us, warns us, often corrects us, but continually matures us. A stagnant faith is cured by daily and sometimes hourly worship of Jesus, our Master. One day our journey to the throne will come to total fruition when we see Him face to face. In fact, one day everyone, whether or not they submit to their Adonai, Master, in this life, will acknowledge that He is King. When that day comes, I'm excited to see Jesus' shining face, and I look forward to praising Him in person.

> And every creature which is in heaven and on the earth and under
> the earth and such as are in the sea, and all that are in them, I heard
> saying: "Blessing and honor and glory and power be to Him who sits
> on the throne, and to the Lamb, forever and ever!" (Revelation 5:13)

Today let's begin the celebration. Let's accept the freedom gifted to us when we approach the throne of our Adonai, Master, not afraid of the fact that we are submitting control to Him. The joy comes in seeing the wonders He works in our life when all praise and honor and control are laid down before the throne during worship.

Journal 2
I WILL WORSHIP AT THE THRONE

- Describe your state of worship. Do you enjoy praising and honoring your Adonai? If not, ask the Lord to give you a heart for worship. Ask Him to show you how He wants you to worship.

- How has your worship changed, if at all, during the course of reading this book?

- There are several areas in the Bible that describe the day that Jesus will return. In your Bible, check out Philippians 2:5–11. I love how this scripture shows us the humble and holy nature of Jesus. Hone in on verses 9–11, which are similar to the verses we discussed from Revelation.

> Therefore God also has highly exalted Him and given Him the name which is above every name, that at the name of Jesus every knee should bow, of those in heaven, and of those on earth, and of those under the earth, and that every tongue should confess that Jesus Christ is Lord, to the glory of God the Father. (Philippians 2:9–11)

• Verse 9 says that Jesus' name is above all. How does that sit with you?

• How can you take a posture of bowing low before Jesus as in verse 10? What about in prayer? Would you feel comfortable kneeling (in privacy) as a way to physically humble yourself before your Master?

• In your own words, how would you "confess" or, rather, express that Jesus Christ is Lord and Master of your life?

• How can you make room for worship in your life every single day? (For example: listening to a worship song on the way to work, making time during lunch break, etc.)

• How can you break out of your comfort zone and develop more expressive worship toward the Lord?

Waiting at the Throne of the King

In the chapters touching on career, dating, and money, we discussed literally waiting on the Lord and the development of patience. I remember my high school computer lab teacher who always responded to my impatience with the old, slow computers by saying, "Patience is a virtue and virtue never hurt you." This annoyed me to no end as I'm naturally not a patient person. Waiting on Adonai means we set aside our desire to rush through life and instead allow Him to fulfill His timing, which is always the best for us anyway.

The same goes with complaining and grumbling in life. I'm willing to bet that our girlfriend Gina is not the only one of us who gripes about her job. I often find myself grumbling if a sweet little old lady is writing out a check at the grocery store instead of quickly swiping a debit card. Griping and complaining, I'm afraid to say, are aspects of my character that I admit need to change. When we complain about our situations, we bring energy into the room that affects those around us. I would hate to be the one who darkens the mood within my team at work because I'm griping about petty issues. And I'm wondering how our poor attitudes and complaining affect the way others see Jesus through us. The negative comments coming out of our mouths blind others to the many good things about our lives that God blesses us with. The people in our lives who need to hear how great our God is are missing that good news when . . .

- ⁒ A complaint about the lack of clothes in our closet disregards how He cares for our every need in addition to our wants.

- ⁒ A complaint about an assignment from our professor disguises a heart that is grateful for a college education.

- ⁒ A conversation full of negative words about a girlfriend covers up the wonderful qualities of her personality and taints the friendship.

In addition to waiting at the throne of our Master Adonai with a patient heart, let's consider also adding to the mix what is called a sacrifice of thanksgiving and praise. This concept of giving God praise as a sacrifice struck me about a year ago and revolutionized my attitude toward God and how He so graciously blesses me.

> Oh, that men would give thanks to the LORD for His goodness, and for His wonderful works to the children of men! Let them sacrifice the sacrifices of thanksgiving, and declare His works with rejoicing. (Psalm 107:21–22)

In the Old Testament the people of God were required to offer many different types of sacrifices in order for God to cleanse them of their sins. These days, when we accept that Jesus died on the cross as a sacrifice for our sins, we're no longer required to perform the rituals of the Old Testament. This doesn't cancel out the teaching of the Old Testament for us as New Testament believers. I look at the phrase "sacrifice of thanksgiving" as still very applicable to my life. The sacrifice comes into play when I praise my Adonai regardless of my mood or inclination to complain. Even when we don't want to say "Thank You, Lord!" we do anyway because we know that He is absolutely due our grateful heart and praise. Hopefully after offering up this sacrifice day after day, even when we don't want to, that practice of praise actually turns into something we want to do. This new attitude bleeds into the rest of our life as we look at our daily stress points with a new frame of reference: looking for the blessings in every situation and offering up thanksgiving to our Adonai.

As we approach the throne and wait on our Adonai daily, we trade in our grumbling and complaining with words that positively affect those around us. I challenge you to look at your daily verbiage and evaluate if there is any negativity in the way you speak. I've learned to address these negative thoughts and complaints by talking straight to God about them first. Instead of ignoring the annoyances in my life that cause my complaining, I discuss them with God, asking Him to give me His perspective. It is God alone who can work through His Holy Spirit in our heart to transform our attitudes about our life. Even though the Lord hates a heart that complains, He does allow us to approach the throne with our feelings, which is more productive than voicing our opinions as complaints. God hears our thoughts and interjects His peace, patience, and joy into the situation. We must be open to seeing our stress points from the perspective of the throne rather than from our own muddied, negative viewpoint.

Let's do just that right now and journal through what is in our heart that we are tempted to complain and grumble about. Spiritual maturity only happens when we know how to take our feelings to the Lord. It is human nature to complain and whine, but a mature woman of God takes her feelings to the throne, talks them through with Him and trades her negative with God's grace.

Journal 3
I WILL WAIT AT THE THRONE OF MY KING

- We did something similar to this in the chapter on self-image, and we don't want to spend too much time focusing on the negative, so take *two* minutes (seriously, time it!) to jot down anything and everything you are complaining about these days. This is how we are going to bring our grumbling straight to the throne.

- Before we take time to journal out a prayer to the Lord regarding our complaints, check out how Paul encouraged the people of Philippi in regard to their nature to grumble and complain.

  Do all things without complaining and disputing, that you may become blameless and harmless, children of God without fault in the midst of a crooked and perverse generation, among whom you shine as lights in the world, holding fast the word of life, so that I may rejoice in the day of Christ that I have not run in vain or labored in vain. (Philippians 2:14–16)

- In light of Philippians 2, take a moment to prayer journal through the list of your complaints and grumbles. Get honest and raw with Adonai about why these things bug you. Only He can change your perspective.

- Philippians 2 encourages us that we will shine like stars when we hold fast to the Word of God and live a life without complaining and disputing. How do you think you can be a light (a positive example of Jesus) when you refrain from complaining and grumbling to your family and to those around you at work, at school, at the gym, etc.?

- Take a few minutes to look up the word *rejoice* in the concordance or index of your Bible. Write out a few of the verses below. Commit to soaking in these verses this week as a replacement for negative thoughts or speech.

Finding Focus on Him Alone

I'm wondering if you identified with my story of turning to earthly things like a bottle of wine rather than releasing my anxiety and stress to my Adonai. Bad days are just part of life. I usually take them in stride and move on. However, this was a very bad day that had me feeling like I was locked in a pressure cooker that was about to explore at any minute. When I evaluated the way I handled that stress, I looked deep down into the dark spaces of my heart to ask myself these questions:

- ❧ Why did I turn to something other than Jesus to release the pressure from a stinky, stressful day?

- ❧ What is it about God's perfect, comforting, life-giving character that I do not understand and instead turn to things like a bottle of wine?

A cold hard truth revealed itself as I pondered my motivations for handling my bad day by drinking wine. We all have stress; that is what this book is filled with, life issues that we all must deal with. The issue with how I dealt with my stress was not about drinking, per se. We've discussed this topic before as it relates to boundaries in chapter 8. The issue was that I didn't turn straight to the Lord for the solution and release of my stress. This is a sin, which I know is a strong word. But it was straight-up sin that I put something (alcohol) above my Lord, Adonai. He has the solution to our problems, but we are only able to receive that solution when we place our focus on the throne of our Master rather than the sin of earthly solutions. None of us are exempt from this proclamation in Romans: "You see, all have sinned, and all their futile attempts to reach God in His glory fail" (Romans 3:23 THE VOICE).

We all fall short of the standards God sets for us. No matter how spiritually mature we are, there will always be times that you and I sin. I hate this about myself. I so badly want to live my life in a pure manner that pleases God all the time. The next two verses in Romans 3 give me assurance that my life is, in fact, right with God.

> Yet they are now saved and set right by His free gift of grace through the redemption available only in Jesus the Anointed. When God set Him up to be the sacrifice—the seat of mercy where sins are atoned through faith—His blood became the demonstration of God's own restorative justice. (Romans 3:24–25 THE VOICE)

I so appreciate the idea of restoration here in Romans 3:25. Jesus restores us and sets us up right back in front of the holy throne when we've fallen short and fallen away from the throne with our sin. The beauty of having our focus set on Jesus is that the more we live in His glorious presence, through every single stress point in our life, our heart changes; our mind conforms to that of His. When we find focus on Him alone, every day, we mold our behavior into daily actions that steer us toward pleasing God rather than indulging our sin.

This spiritual maturity comes with a day in and day out, continual movement toward the throne. The moment we pull away our focus on Him, we slide backward from the throne toward our own sinful inclination. A spiritually mature heart is one that recognizes when it acts against God's commands and owns up to it right away. I've learned that I cannot let my sin sit on my conscience, for it festers and I continue in the sin, though I know it is wrong. Soon, I begin to live with this anger in my heart that reflects something off-kilter in my life, that I'm not right with God.

We often think we can't return back to the throne due to this guilty conscience, but this conviction is actually the Holy Spirit nudging us back toward the King. Reality check, friends: with arms wide open, our Lord and Master is ready, willing, and capable of freeing us from our sin. We don't have to live in bondage to our actions, addictions, emotions . . . sin.

I would like you to find a quiet space right now. It doesn't matter if you are in the middle of the lunchroom at work or in the middle of an apartment full of noisy roommates, find some quiet spot where you can take some time to search your heart and sit at the throne and focus on your King. For me, this is often in my car before I walk into work. I turn my phone on silent, turn off the radio, and sit with my Lord, pen and pad in hand and my Bible open. Find your place and journal through the questions below. Let's get real about our sin, for there is great freedom in handing our junk over to the King who is strong and mighty to save.

> The LORD your God in your midst, The Mighty One, will save; He will rejoice over you with gladness, He will quiet you with His love, He will rejoice over you with singing. (Zephaniah 3:16–18)

Journal 4

I FIND FOCUS ON HIM ALONE

- Journal through anything on your heart that you know is not pleasing God.

_____

_____

_____

- Journal through these same questions that I asked of myself that stressful day.

Why did I turn to something other than Jesus to release the pressure from a stinky, stressful day?

_____

_____

_____

What is it about God's perfect, comforting, life-giving character in which I do not understand and instead turn to things like _____?

_____

_____

_____

- Flip to Psalm 42 and soak in this psalm by reading through it several times.

- Pick out a verse within Psalm 42 that speaks to you about God's forgiveness and restoration from sin when we are in the middle of life's stress. Write out this verse here.

- What is it about this verse that encourages you the most? How can you live out this verse today?

Stress Diverted

Take a glance back at our working definition of spiritual maturity. I included in this definition an aspect of questioning God that is specifically for you as a 20-something. This is naturally a decade of exploration, inquisition, and plainly figuring life out for yourself. I wonder what questions you've asked in regard to your faith. I wonder if you have struggled with certain passages in the Bible that the world often considers controversial. The fact that God's Word says that there is only one way to heaven via Jesus Christ causes strife and questioning in so many hearts. Because so much of our world declares many routes to God, many ways and actions to end up in heaven, it is difficult as Christian women not to question what the truth is. This is completely acceptable to God. You are allowed to ponder and wrestle with parts of the Bible that might not make sense to you. All throughout the Psalms, David worked through His issues with the Lord.

We are able to approach the King in worship, in waiting at the throne, and in focusing on Him and bringing our questions of faith. I hope that you have already explored your questions and journaled through them with the Lord throughout this book. Oh how I hope that He's spoken to your need to inquire and showed you that it is okay to take anything and everything to Him, even the issues and questions you struggle with.

I encourage you to explore, inquire, and question the Master, Adonai, with white knuckles. When we hold tight to Jesus, we should grasp Him so tight our knuckles turn white. These white knuckles aid us in asking God the tough stuff without walking astray during the exploration. Our white knuckles keep us right in His presence rather than flying off the handle and following the world's fleeting teachings regarding faith. Jesus is not afraid of our questions; He knows that He is Ultimate Truth. Ask away with a tight fist gripping the hand of your Master. Let Him walk you through your questions and guide you as you ponder. As you journey with your Adonai, the special pearls of biblical truth that He speaks specifically into your questioning heart will stay with you for life, made all the more meaningful because you walked with Him through the questions.

Let us close this final chapter with a verse that gives us a rich visual of what it means to approach the throne of our King of Kings. We've explored this verse in our journey to the throne together, but it's a meaningful passage that is worth ending our final chapter with. Let the image burn into your mind as you live out your faith in every single stress point in your life. He is the answer, my friend. He welcomes you to His throne anytime, anyplace, and with any type of junk you deal with. He is also eager for your thanksgiving and praise; oh how He is so worthy of your worship.

> So let us step bold to the throne of grace, where we can find mercy and grace to help when we need it most. (Hebrews 4:16 THE VOICE)

Journal 5

I WILL LAY IT ALL DOWN BEFORE THE THRONE

- *Father God, I boldly approach Your throne with assurance that You welcome me with open arms . . .*

- *You, my Master, are my only way to freedom and a life of fulfillment. I submit to You specifically in these areas . . .*

- *Thank You, my Adonai, for the love and freedom You pour out over me. I see Your freedom in these areas of my life . . .*

- *Show me, oh Lord, areas of my life that I've yet to hand over to You as I come to Your glorious throne . . .*

*Go to **www.liveitoutblog.com/stress-point** to watch*
a video from Sarah on this chapter's Stress Point!

CONCLUSION
WRAP UP AND DE-STRESS

I'm so honored that you joined me in talking through ten stress points—what a journey. As I wrote this book, with every keystroke I had you in mind and the ultimate goal of encouraging you to see that Jesus is King of Kings in every single area of your life. As I've worked through each chapter, I've realized that I, too, have much work to do to hand over my stress to Him. I'm a work in progress. There's always something new in my life to lay down before the throne of the King. As we have journaled together and worked through Bible study questions, I so hope that . . .

ᔕ when the bills pile up and it's difficult to get your budget in order, you'll let your King claim it *Mine*.

ᔕ when your boyfriend gives you mixed signals and your heart is stretched and tattered, you'll let your King claim it *Mine*.

ᔕ when you just can't drag yourself one more day to your job and the prospects of a new one are slim, you'll let your King claim it *Mine*.

• How has Jesus, your King, put His claim over your life and your stress points after you've spent some time with Him via this book?

_____

_____

_____

As a way to conclude this book together, I really want to ensure that our time together was not in vain. Let's make sure this time spent transforms the way we live out the Kingship of Christ. Take some time, maybe a few days, to sift through each chapter and record a few key points that you've learned.

ଓ What are some ways your King spoke straight to your heart?

ଓ What are some things you will do differently from here on out?

I don't know about you, but I don't want to go through life incapable of being stretched and changed and I would hate for you to read through these ten chapters, close the book, and just move on. Let this wrap-up serve as a reference for the future. Come back to the notes you will jot down in the pages that follow, and remember little pearls of truth that can guide you in your career, money, dating, relationships, and all of your stress points. This is a place for you to reflect and bring it all together.

STRESS POINT 1
Career: Wishing for That Dream Job

NAME OF GOD: EL ELYON, GOD MOST HIGH

• How does this name of God speak to you about your career?

_____

_____

• Write out one of the Bible verses in this chapter that stood out to you regarding your career.

_____

_____

_____

• What is one way you can live out the Kingship of Christ in your career?

_____

_____

_____

244

STRESS POINT 2

Self-Image: Comfortable in My Own Skin

NAME OF GOD: MAJESTIC KING

- How does this name of God speak to you about your self-image?

_____

_____

- Write out one of the Bible verses in this chapter that stood out to you regarding your self-image.

_____

_____

_____

- What is one way you can live out the Kingship of Christ with your self-image?

_____

_____

_____

STRESS POINT 3

Body Image: I Heart the Skinny Mirror

NAME OF GOD: ELOHIM, OUR CREATOR

- How does this name of God speak to you about your body image?

_____

_____

- Write out one of the Bible verses in this chapter that stood out to you regarding your body image.

_____

_____

_____

- What is one way you can live out the Kingship of Christ with your body image?

_____

_____

_____

STRESS POINT 4
Love/Dating Part 1: He Is Just That into You

NAME OF GOD: IMMANUEL, GOD WITH US

- How does this name of God speak to you about your dating relationships? (If you aren't in a relationship, journal through how this might affect future relationships.)

_____

_____

- Write out one of the Bible verses in this chapter that stood out to you regarding your dating relationships.

_____

_____

- What is one way you can live out the Kingship of Christ with your dating relationships?

STRESS POINT 5
Love/Dating Part 2: Quite Intense

NAME OF GOD: DIVINE, JEALOUS GOD

- How does this name of God speak to you about your intense relationships? (If you aren't in a relationship, journal through how this might affect future relationships.)

- Write out one of the Bible verses in this chapter that stood out to you regarding your intense relationships.

- What is one way you can live out the Kingship of Christ with your intense relationships?

STRESS POINT 6

Friends and Family: Save the Drama

NAME OF GOD: ETERNAL GOD

- How does this name of God speak to you about your relationships with friends and family?

- Write out one of the Bible verses in this chapter that stood out to you regarding relationships with friends and family.

- What is one way you can live out the Kingship of Christ with your relationships with friends and family?

STRESS POINT 7

Money: Retail Therapy Doesn't Cut It

NAME OF GOD: EL SHADDAI, HE IS MORE THAN ENOUGH

• How does this name of God speak to you about your money?

• Write out one of the Bible verses in this chapter that stood out to you regarding your money.

• What is one way you can live out the Kingship of Christ with your money?

STRESS POINT 8

Stepping Out on Your Own: Miss Independent

NAME OF GOD: OUR HIDING PLACE

• How does this name of God speak to you about stepping out on your own in the world? (If you are not yet at this point in your life, journal through what this would look like in the future.)

- Write out one of the Bible verses in this chapter that stood out to you regarding stepping out on your own.

_____

_____

_____

- What is one way you can live out the Kingship of Christ while you step out on your own in the world?

_____

_____

_____

STRESS POINT 9
Making a Difference:
I Can Make a Difference (Start a Ripple)

NAME OF GOD: JEHOVAH-NISSI, THE LORD IS MY BANNER

- How does this name of God speak to you about making a difference in your world?

_____

_____

- Write out one of the Bible verses in this chapter that stood out to you regarding making a difference.

_____

_____

- What is one way you can live out the Kingship of Christ while make a difference in your world?

_____

_____

_____

STRESS POINT 10
Spiritual Maturity: Growing Through the Stress

NAME OF GOD: ADONAI, OUR MASTER

- How does this name of God speak to you about your growth and spiritual maturity?

_____

_____

- Write out one of the Bible verses in this chapter that stood out to you regarding spiritual maturity.

_____

_____

_____

- What is one way you can live out the Kingship of Christ and grow closer to Jesus?

_____

_____

_____

STRESS POINT SURVIVAL GROUP LEADER GUIDE

I'm excited that you've taken the step toward leading a small group of women to live out the Kingship of Christ together and learn from one another. If you are a 20-something with a desire to lead your peers and grow together, I want to say thank you. It's not easy to make time in your life to prepare and lead. It's also a bit scary to think that you will lead your friends through this book and discuss the Bible. I want to hug you this very moment in gratitude that you've stepped forward to journey with your friends in a Stress Point Survival Group. If you are a mentor to 20-somethings and desire to do life with your younger girlfriends by working through this book, I also want to say thank you. These young adult women need your wisdom and coaching and I know it means the world that you set time aside in your schedule to hang out.

My main goal for you, in addition to the obvious goal that you, too, would learn and grow, is that you do not burn out as a leader. I hope that this book will be a springboard for groups of young adult women to meet regularly and dig through the Bible to find truth applicable to everyday life. Because I want you to be encouraged to continue to lead, please hear me say that leading Stress Point should be impactful as well as low-key for you and your group. Let's all say this together: **I will not stress out over leading Stress Point!** (Did you really say that aloud? I sure hope so!)

Because this is a low-key and low-maintenance Survival Group, I want to take some time to lay out a few helpful hints for gathering a group. These are some tips I've learned over my years of ministry with 20-somethings. This is in no way a "must do" list, but a few things to think about if you've never lead a small group before. In addition, I will break down each chapter into a main theme and give you a few more discussion questions to talk through with your group.

It is my hope that your group members will learn to trust each other and cultivate an atmosphere of authenticity. This starts with the leader, so prayerfully consider how you personally add to the culture of authenticity with your group. Please don't feel like you need to know all of the answers. It is okay to say, "I don't know, but I will look into it." If one of your girls brings up a difficult topic that you don't know how to respond to, continue the conversation to garner the opinions of others in the group. Then, I suggest talking to your pastor or women's ministry leader to get their thoughts. No one looks down on someone who admits she doesn't know. In fact, your group will see you as one who cares about getting to the truth if you commit to finding out an answer and reporting back at the next group meeting. The important thing is that you all prayerfully come before your King, get to a deep discussion based on Scripture, and listen to each others' thoughts and feelings.

Helpful Hints:

- ℰ Wherever you decide to hold your Survival Group, set it up with comfortable couches, chairs, and pillows. This is easy to do at a house, but takes a bit more intention if you are meeting at a church or other building.

- ℰ Keep the group to no more than ten women. It helps the flow of conversation when everyone feels like they have a voice and are not lost in a big group.

- ℰ Don't feel like you need to have a fancy food setup. I've spent hours preparing snacks for my girls and they end up in Tupperware and in my fridge—not eaten. Simple coffee, sodas, and water are really the maximum you need to set out.

- ℰ Though you want to keep the group free-flowing and structured lightly, set a specific start and finish time for each meeting in order to be respectful of everyone's time.

ଔ Collect the e-mail addresses and phone numbers of everyone that signs up. Then, the day of your group, send out an e-mail and text message to your members as a friendly reminder. You might feel like this is overdoing it, but everyone likes to be reminded during their busy days.

ଔ A great way to handle prayer requests and allow the women to engage with each other is to hand out index cards and have everyone write down one prayer request, their name, e-mail address, and phone number. Then put the cards in a pile and ask everyone to pick one random card. Then, throughout the week, ask everyone to touch base with the person on their card to offer encouragement and prayer.

ଔ Encourage your group to do the journal questions for each chapter. I purposefully didn't call these sections "homework," but these journals solidify the concepts in each chapter and are crucial to growth and engagement with the Lord. In addition to the Real, Raw, and Relevant questions that will follow in this Leader Guide, these journal questions can offer starting points for in-depth discussions. Be sure not to discourage those who do not complete their journals, though.

I want you to know that I'm so honored that you chose to use *Stress Point* for your small group. This is not a task to be taken lightly, but know that the Lord will bless you greatly for taking on this responsibility. Here is what I am praying specifically for you as a leader:

Father God, I thank You for calling this leader to guide her group of friends through Stress Point. Oh how I pray that they will see You as their King of Kings in a very real way as they work through all of these life issues. Cover this sweet leader with Your guidance and grace. Show her that You are glorified because she stepped up to led her friends toward Your majestic throne. Give her holy confidence and protect her from anything that will discourage or block her during this journey. I'm so very excited to see how You, our King, will move in the lives of these women. In Jesus' name, Amen!

I've broken down each *Stress Point* chapter to give you more discussion suggestions to move the conversation along. These discussion questions will give you a starting point for your group to share transparently about each chapter's theme. Each chapter outline will have one main point, The Main Thing, to help you grasp the big takeaway for that stress point. These are followed by The Real, The Raw, and The Relevant discussion questions. Please don't feel like you have to use all of these discussion questions as there might be some conversations that arise based on the chapter journal questions, and you may run out of time.

CHAPTER I
Stress Point: Career

The Main Thing: El Elyon, God Most High (Psalm 7:17)

No matter where you are in your career, living the dream job or not, God Most High has all of the twists and turns worked out. We must make Him our Wish, our focus.

The Real: What if your original dream job doesn't turn out to be all it's cracked up to be, yet you have no idea what you'd rather do?

The Raw: How often do you think of turning to your King with questions and worries over your career? What keeps you from allowing Him to give you direction? Do you trust Him with your job?

The Relevant: On page 21 Sarah said, "Keep in mind that most people in their early twenties don't step off the college graduation platform directly into their six-figure dream job. Most of us have to pay our dues, putting in time in jobs that give us meaningful experience but barely give us enough money to pay the bills! This period may be considered almost a rite of passage, not to mention an important moment in which to practice waiting on God and submitting to His timing for our career path." Does this frustrate you in any way? Do you let your dreams and career aspirations distract you from having a relationship with Jesus and following His path?

CHAPTER 2
Stress Point: Self-Image

The Main Thing: Majestic King (Psalm 8:3–5)

We were not created to obsess over being grounded or over finding who we are. Instead, we were created to worship and immerse our entire self in the Lord who is full of glory and majesty. Wrapping our self and our identity in Jesus takes time and effort on our part, and that includes worshiping Him for this majesty and recognizing how our self fits into the concept.

The Real: Sarah talks about living our life authentically, even when we are unsure and insecure. This means sharing our struggles with our friends, both online and offline. She gave us the Facebook Challenge (pages 42–43). Did you accept this challenge yet? What are your thoughts on how being authentic allows for others to share in our struggles and find encouragement?

The Raw: Sarah shared a very raw memory from junior high. It is easy to allow hurtful memories to define us. It is also easy to allow the opinions of others get in the way of the truth of who we are in Jesus. Dig into your response to Journal 4 in this chapter, and share some verses you jotted down.

The Relevant: What are your thoughts on Sarah's analysis of "Firework" by Katy Perry? How do you see culture encouraging us to make our name famous rather than lifting up the name of our Majestic King? What are your thoughts on how Jesus sets the ultimate example in Philippians 2:9–11?

CHAPTER 3
Stress Point: Body Image

The Main Thing: Elohim, Our Creator (Genesis 1)

With a heart full of admiration of our King, our Creator, we must not worship the creation—obsess about our body—but rather worship at the glorious throne of the Creator. For when our energy is spent picking and prodding at our self-perceived flaws, we distract our worship from the One who painted our eyes blue, who tinted our skin a perfect shade of olive, who sculpted our hips with beautiful curves.

The Real: In Journal 1, Sarah encouraged us to get real with our body issues. In an effort to see we aren't alone in our body hatred, dish out loud some of your personal issues with your body. Does it help to see that others, whom you might very well admire, also have struggles with their body image?

The Raw: Do you equate your body with the majestic and amazing creation of our Elohim? Why is it so hard to accept our bodies?

The Relevant: Together as a group read Colossians 3:23 (NIV):

> Whatever you do, work at it with all your heart, as working for the Lord, not for men.

• How do you think this verse applies to how you personally treat your body in order to best serve the Lord?

_____

_____

• What is one way you will take care of the creation, your body, this week?

_____

_____

CHAPTER 4
Stress Point: Love/Dating Part 1

(Note to leader: If women in your group are not in a dating relationship, please encourage them to continue through the next two chapters and file away these very important truths for godly relationships.)

The Main Thing: Immanuel, God with Us

> You shall be a crown of beauty in the hand of the LORD, and a royal diadem in the hand of your God. You shall no more be termed Forsaken, and your land shall no more be termed Desolate, but you shall be called My Delight Is In Her. (Isaiah 62:3–4 ESV)

Through every stage of life—the good, the bad, and the ugly—God is with us. This includes our romantic life. What girl doesn't want to feel as though she's the only one in the room, the most beautiful, absolutely captivating to someone? Our Immanuel makes this a reality.

The Real: Describe your ideal guy (how he treats you, how you relate to each other, what you have in common, his personality, his relationship with the Lord, etc.). What are the challenges to finding a godly man?

The Raw: Sex and dating go hand in hand these days. Based on Journal 3, read through Ephesians 5:1–3 (MSG):

> Watch what God does, and then you do it, like children who learn proper behavior from their parents. Mostly what God does is love you. . . . Love like that. Don't allow love to turn into lust, setting off a downhill slide into sexual promiscuity.

* How do you see sex before marriage as a downhill slide? How does it affect the relationship in a negative way?

The Relevant: What are some ways we, as friends, can encourage each other to cling tightly to our Immanuel? How can we hold each other accountable to keeping godly relationships with guys?

CHAPTER 5
Stress Point: Love/Dating, Part 2

The Main Thing: Divine, Jealous God (Deuteronomy 4:24)

To worship our King with our intense relationships is to bring to the throne the passionate, romantic feelings that swell in our heart and oftentimes overwhelm us to the point where we worship the guy in our life instead of our Divine, Jealous God.

The Real: In light of the world's definition of *jealous*, what are your thoughts on the fact that we serve a Divine, Jealous God?

The Raw: Talk through the illustration of the triangle on page 104.

The Relevant: On page 114 Sarah says, "If a certain part of your relationship (sex or anything else) hinders your constant focus at the throne of the King, it needs to be eliminated. Through prayer, take some time to set boundaries in your physical relationship with your man. These boundaries are different for each couple because each couple has different triggers that cause them to move into territory that is no longer obedient."

• Though they might be hard to swallow, what are some boundaries that need to be set in an intense relationship?

- What are the challenges of setting boundaries (physical and emotional) in intense relationships?

- What positives do you see in putting up these boundaries?

CHAPTER 6
Stress Point: Friends and Family

The Main Thing: Eternal God (Psalm 93)

When it comes to family, worshiping at the throne of the King means we celebrate these special people and don't waste the gift that they are to us we go about our everyday lives. Though flawed and only human, these people are used by God to give us a slight glimpse of one aspect of His character: He is the Eternal God. Those in our lives who know our dirt and can see into the deep, dark crevasses of our hearts yet still love us and refuse to leave us reflect the love of our God who will absolutely never walk away.

Love your God with all your heart, soul, and mind. Let Jesus, the Eternal God, pour His never-ending acceptance into your heart so you are free from striving for the acceptance of your friends and family.

The Real: Sarah asked us to write out our definition of a "normal" family with the thought that there is no real normal. Discuss your definition.

The Raw: Talk about the challenges of respecting your family's new dynamic now that you are an adult. What are the advantages of this, and how does it glorify the Lord?

The Relevant: Work through Journal 3 (page 136) and discuss these verses regarding Eternal God in light of friendships.

* In what ways do we often live in a Christian bubble, secluded from the non-Christians in our life? What is one way we can get out of that bubble and "mix it up"?

CHAPTER 7

Stress Point: Money

The Main Thing: El Shaddai, He Is More than Enough (Ephesians 3:17–19)

Continuous cycles of wants and needs repeat indefinitely. *El Shaddai* translates into an amazing phrase: "God is the all-sufficient One" or "God Almighty." I personally like to take this word *Shaddai* one step further: Jesus, my El Shaddai, is over the top; He's more than sufficient, more than enough for me. And He's more than enough for you, too, my friend.

The Real: What is your definition of a void? Get real about specific voids in your life and how you attempt to fill them.

* How do the ways you attempt to fill your voids fall short?

The Raw: What does it mean to you that Jesus, your El Shaddai, is more than enough? That He can give you all the fullness you need?

• Read John 10:10. How does this encourage you?

_____

_____

The Relevant: Work through the spending experiment Sarah poses in Journal 4. Talk about the various guilty pleasures that you all fall prey to. How much money is spent monthly? How can you hold each other accountable to regularly evaluating your spending based on filling up on Jesus rather than stuff?

CHAPTER 8
Stress Point: Stepping Out on Your Own

The Main Thing: Our Hiding Place (Psalm 32:7)

To explore this stress point, we will look at the feelings of apprehension about moving out on our own and how to fully live out our new role as Miss Independent. A true woman who clings to her King, Jesus, knows that she is never truly independent, but completely dependent on the Lord for guidance, direction, protection, and emotional support.

The Real: Talk through Journal 2 and the concept of our safety nets. How do these people lift us up? How do they hamper us from relying solely on our Hiding Place, Jesus?

The Raw: On page 176 Sarah says, "It might be a terrifying leap out of our safety nets, but this leap gratifies the deep desire to hold tightly to One who covers all of our fears and anxieties that might bubble up when stepping out on our own."

• How do you see stepping out on your own as a way to grow closer to the Lord, your Hiding Place? Is it difficult to trust Him with this step?

• Do Life Mechanics freak you out? If so, what are ways that you can hand over control and fear of these Life Mechanics to find strength to deal with them?

The Relevant: Sarah discusses the fruit of the Spirit in relation to setting personal boundaries for how we live. Read through Galatians 5:22. What are your thoughts on this concept? How can you use the fruit of the Spirit as a guideline for your behavior?

CHAPTER 9
Stress Point: Making a Difference

The Main Thing: Jehovah-Nissi, The Lord Is My Banner (Psalm 60:4–5)

Our grand plans and schemes to do great things for God fall flat if we think that we can dream and plan and then expect God to graciously join in and bless us. A major paradigm shift occurs when we realize that God is already doing amazing things around us. If we take some time to ask Him to reveal an area where He is moving and shaking things up, then and only then can we join in with our God-given talents and affect change.

The Real: What is your desire to make a difference in your world? Why is it that our generation has such a deep-seated desire to affect change?

The Raw: On page 198 Sarah discusses the taxi versus the subway. How does this illustration change your view on jumping in and making a difference in the world around you? How does this passage in John sit with you in light of this illustration?

> My Father has been working until now, and I have been working. . . . Most assuredly, I say to you, the Son can do nothing of Himself, but what He sees the Father do; for whatever He does, the Son also does in like manner. For the Father loves the Son, and shows Him all things that He Himself does; and He will show Him greater works than these, that you may marvel. (John 5:17, 19–20)

The Relevant: As a group, brainstorm ways that you all can make a difference in your own backyard. It doesn't have to be elaborate or hard to plan. Come up with one idea from that list and make a concrete plan to do this project as a group within the next few months.

CHAPTER 10
Stress Point: Spiritual Maturity

The Main Thing: Adonai, Our Master (Philippians 2:9–11)

Our definition of a spiritually mature woman is someone who

- ∞ is in continual motion toward the throne of her King.

- ∞ has a heart that sees its faults and readily owns up to its mistakes, knowing she is forgiven because Jesus loved her so much He died on the cross for her.

- ∞ questions Jesus and evaluates her faith every day with assurance that questions are healthy and acceptable.

ભ habitually opens her Bible with reverence and desires that the Word of God flow into every area of her life. She never ceases to spend time with Him, and if she does neglect this quality time, she knows she is always welcome right back to the throne.

ભ loves others more than herself because she knows we are all created and loved by our almighty King.

The Real: On page 222 Sarah says, "We will begin to find freedom in this name of the Lord—Adonai, Master—when we worship daily in the freedom of relenting completely to His reign and control over our lives, over all of our stress points."

Over the course of this study, how have you found freedom and maturity when releasing your stress points over to your Master?

The Raw: What do you think about taking a posture of bowing low before our High and Almighty Master?

Rather than a degrading posture, we are actually lifted up high by our King and Master when we bow low before Him. Thoughts?

The Relevant: Look over Journal 4 together and read through Philippians 2:14–16 as a group.

The passage encourages us that we will shine like stars when we hold fast to the Word of God and live a life without complaining and disputing. How do you think you can be a light (a positive example of Jesus) when you refrain from complaining and grumbling to your family and to those around you at work, at school, at the gym, etc.?

Suggestion: Throw a Stress Point Survival Party

After your group finishes and "survives" the Stress Point Survival Group, wouldn't it be fun to throw a de-stress party? Have everyone bring their favorite snack to share and watch a good ole' chick flick. If your group has grown really close and comfortable with each other, maybe even have a dance party or play Just Dance on the Wii. Be sure to have your camera ready (no posting pics on Facebook, though!). There's nothing better to relieve stress than a night filled with laughter and good food with your girl-friends. Oh how I wish I could be there in person with you! (I'm a *champion* at Just Dance 2 on the Wii.) Be sure to check in on the Stress Point Web site, and if you've got permission from your group members, you can even share funny stories or pictures from the party! Visit www.liveitoutblog. com/stress-point.

EXTRA RESOURCES
APPENDIX

Because I do not claim expertise on all of the stress points we covered together, I want to share some great books and Web sites that will give you more insight and wisdom. I dearly love books, and some of these are my personal recommendations and favorite go-to reads. Others are great Web sites for inspiration and guidance. I hope you enjoy perusing these books and clicking through the Web sites!

STRESS POINT: CAREER

Climbing the Ladder in Stilettos: 10 Strategies for Stepping Up to Success and Satisfaction at Work by Lynette Lewis

STRESS POINT: SELF-IMAGE

A Confident Heart: How to Stop Doubting Yourself and Live in the Security of God's Promises by Renee Swope

STRESS POINT: BODY IMAGE

Michelle Myers, fitness expert, *Michelle Myers Online* (blog): http://michellemyersonline.com/

The Look That Kills: An Anorexic's Addiction to Control by Michelle Myers

STRESS POINT: LOVE/DATING

Not Another Dating Book: A Devotional Guide to All Your Relationships by Renee Fisher

Entrusting the Key: From Serial Dating to Joyful Waiting by Ali Smith

Real Marriage: The Truth about Sex, Friendship, and Life Together by Mark Driscoll and Grace Driscoll

STRESS POINT: FRIENDS AND FAMILY

Victoria Jenkins and Elisse Kipe, *Biblical Friendship* (blog): http://biblical-friendship.com/

God, Grace, and Girlfriends: Adventures in Faith and Friendship by Mary R. Snyder

STRESS POINT: MONEY

The Total Money Makeover: A Proven Plan for Financial Fitness by Dave Ramsey

Get Naked: Stripping Down to Money and Marriage by Derek Sisterhen

STRESS POINT: MAKING A DIFFERENCE

Don't Waste Your Life by John Piper

STRESS POINT: SPIRITUAL MATURITY

(Note: There are so many great books on faith, theology and growth. These are a few selections that personally made an impact on my life.)

How Now Shall We Live? by Charles Colson, Nancy Pearcey, and Harold Fickett

The Pursuit of God by A. W. Tozer

Believing God: Experiencing a Fresh Explosion of Faith by Beth Moore

Jesus Calling: Enjoying Peace in His Presence by Sarah Young

NOTES

1. Renee Swope, *A Confident Heart: How to Stop Doubting Yourself and Live in the Security of God's Promises* (Grand Rapids, MI: Revell, 2011).

2. Taken from the SELF website, www.self.com.

3. *Merriam-Webster's Collegiate Dictionary*, 11th ed., (Springfield, MA: Merriam-Webster, 2003), s.v. "majesty."

4. Renee Swope, *A Confident Heart*, 112.

5. Michelle Myers, "Discovering Your Happy Weight," Michelle Myers Online (blog), October 26, 2011, http://michellemyersonline.com/2011/10/26/discovering-your-happy-weight/.

6. John and Stasi Eldredge, *Captivating Study Guide: Unveiling The Mystery of a Woman's Soul* (Nashville, TN: Thomas Nelson, 2007), 34.

7. *Merriam-Webster's Collegiate Dictionary*, 11th ed., (Springfield, MA: Merriam-Webster, 2003), s.v. "zeal."

8. Sarah Young, *Jesus Calling: Enjoying Peace in His Presence* (Nashville, TN: Thomas Nelson, 2004), 259.

9. John Piper, *Don't Waste Your Life* (Wheaton, IL: Crossway Books, 2003), 43.

ABOUT PROVERBS 31 MINISTRIES

If you were inspired by *Stress Point* and yearn to deepen your own personal relationship with Jesus Christ, I encourage you to connect with Proverbs 31 Ministries. Proverbs 31 Ministries exists to be a trusted friend who will take you by the hand and walk by your side, leading you one step closer to the heart of God through:

- ∞ She Seeks, online weekly inspirational entries specifically for 20-somethings
- ∞ Encouragement for Today, online daily devotions
- ∞ The *P31 Woman* monthly magazine
- ∞ Daily radio program
- ∞ Books and resources
- ∞ Dynamic speakers with life-changing messages
- ∞ Online Communities
- ∞ Gather and Grow groups

To learn more about Proverbs 31 Ministries visit www.proverbs31.org.